Golf Claps for *The Putting*

"I've known Sam Hunter for a good numb[...]
have regularly read his devotionals, which [...]
ers to improve our walk with the Lord. I r[...]
and Sam's are my favorites. They seem to me to be something along the
line of two-minute sermons that are hard-hitting reminders to keep on
being totally committed to the Lord, patching up items in our lives that
need work...

Truthfully, I appreciate the regular push. In spite of my dozens of published books, once I even wrote to Sam and told him that I wished I could write as well as he did! I'd recommend Sam's book for believers who want similarly to be pressed to keep moving forward for the Lord."

Gary R. Habermas, Distinguished Research Professor & Chair,
Dept. of Philosophy, Liberty University and Theological Seminary

"It's been my privilege to know Sam Hunter for almost three decades now, not only to know him as a friend in ministry, but also to see him through the eyes of mutual friends, of his sisters, his Mom and Dad, and his hometown folks. The privilege is that God has allowed me to watch him grow as a man, as a friend, as a Christian, to see how God has led him through rough and smooth patches to shape in him a Christ-formed heart and mind.

I have loved these Putting Green pieces as they were coming forth as e-mail devotions, and I'm thrilled that they are now collected in this form for sharing with others. This is true food and drink for people who are looking for daily help along the way of Christian growth. Thank you, Sam, for sharing your life and yourself in this way."

Rev. Dr. Mark E. Durrett, Eastminster Presbyterian Church,
Columbia, South Carolina

"Filled with common sense and hope, Sam Hunter's *The Putting Green Devotional* offers insight and advice that may steer the confused, perplexed, and straying twenty-first century individual toward a more meaningful, consistent, and rewarding existence."

George Singleton, author of *Stray Decorum*
John C. Cobb Endowed Chair in the Humanities, Wofford College
Finalist, Southeastern Independent Book Assoc. Fiction Book of the Year

"Sam Hunter has assembled a treasure chest of spiritual insights in his 'short game tips.' Each one is proven wisdom that will keep you out of the sand traps seductively set by the world, the flesh, and God's Adversary. Taken together with the Holy Spirit as your caddie, they will allow you to wisely read the spiritual contours of life's greens.

These spiritual gems will also improve your grip and encourage you to let go of the false narratives that may be keeping you from consistently achieving par in your spiritual life."

Doug Greenwold, Senior Teaching Fellow, *Preserving Bible Times*,
Author of *Making Disciples Jesus' Way*

The Putting Green Devotional
Improving Your Life's Short Game

Sam Hunter

High Bridge Books
New York

Contents

Introduction ix
Round 1: Priorities 1
    Hole 1: "Good" Distractions 3
    Hole 2: Self-Seeking or Seeking First? 5
    Hole 3: Stop & Think! 7
    Hole 4: Finding Life 9
    Hole 5: Excuse Me 10
    Hole 6: It Can't Mean That! 12
    Hole 7: My Trust Factor 14
    Hole 8: Surprises 15
    Hole 9: Preoccupied! 17
    Hole 10: Superman 19
    Hole 11: New Beginnings 21
    Hole 12: I Want 23
    Hole 13: My Wants, His Wants 25
    Hole 14: Press On 27
    Hole 15: Saying "Yes" to the Right Things 28
    Hole 16: Distracted! 30
    Hole 17: Focus on Jesus 32
    Hole 18: One Day 34
Round 2: Grace 37
    Hole 1: Amazing Grace 39
    Hole 2: Pretty Good, but Good Enough? 41
    Hole 3: Insanity or Transformation? 43
    Hole 4: Rhythm 45
    Hole 5: He's a Great Dad! 47
    Hole 6: Diva to Disciple 49
    Hole 7: I Got Your Back 51
    Hole 8: Grace Trumps Your Resume 53
    Hole 9: Shame on You! 54
    Hole 10: Changed 56
    Hole 11: B.A.G.G. 58
    Hole 12: The Finest of Wines 60
    Hole 13: Claim It 62
    Hole 14: Whoa, Easy Now 64
    Hole 15: For You – With You – Before You 66
    Hole 16: Free or Slave? 68
    Hole 17: Quicksand 70

Hole 18: Gifted...72

Round 3: Humility 75

Hole 1: *Me* Christianity..77
Hole 2: Deny Yourself..79
Hole 3: The Resume...81
Hole 4: Garden Battle 83
Hole 5: Care – Free...85
Hole 6: Changed & Grateful..87
Hole 7: Rewards 89
Hole 8: A Yard Sale of the Heart...91
Hole 9: I'm Okay, You're Okay?...93
Hole 10: The Hardest Thing..94
Hole 11: The Journey..96
Hole 12: Green Lights – Red Lights...98
Hole 13: The Big Head 100
Hole 14: Authorized 102
Hole 15: My Way or the Highway.. 104
Hole 16: Not Weak, but Meek... 106
Hole 17: A Story of Meek Strength... 108
Hole 18: Bankrupt!.. 110

Round 4: Integrity... 113

Hole 1: Shortcuts 115
Hole 2: What Were You Thinking? 117
Hole 3: Satan's Opening Strategy Session................................... 119
Hole 4: The Narrow Road.. 121
Hole 5: Feeling or Thinking? 123
Hole 6: Desires of the Eyes or of the Heart?.............................. 124
Hole 7: Narrowing Gates – Expanding Life 125
Hole 8: The Mind Melt 127
Hole 9: My Treasure Made Me Do It.. 129
Hole 10: Guard Rails... 130
Hole 11: Guardrail Specifications... 132
Hole 12: High-Five or Utter Contempt?..................................... 134
Hole 13: The Good Life 136
Hole 14: Master Money... 138
Hole 15: Tempted!—The Hot Cookie 140
Hole 16: Esau 142
Hole 17: The Tyranny of Busyness 144
Hole 18: Sin & Other Fun Things... 146

Acknowledgements

I have gained much clarity and insight into the Holy Scriptures from reading the works of Dallas Willard, C.S. Lewis, Charles Stanley, and his son, Andy Stanley. My daily reading of Oswald Chambers' *My Utmost For His Highest* has also added significantly to my understanding of God's message. Also, I must give credit to the men at *Search Ministries*, whose teaching concepts and ideas are creative and impacting.

To these Godly authors and speakers, I owe a debt of gratitude. It is quite likely you will find their ideas throughout these Putting Greens. Any repeating of their words without specific credit is certainly unintentional, so I am hereby giving them most of the credit at the start.

I would like to thank my editor and publicist, Darren Shearer at High Bridge Books, without whom this would still be a stack of individual Putting Green devotionals sitting on my desk. I handed Darren 300 Putting Greens and said, "You do something with these." And he has, in the most excellent of ways.

Introduction

If you ever go to a PGA Tour event and watch professional golfers practice at the range, you'll notice that the best players spend most of their time perfecting their shortest shots. In golf, the 3-yard putt counts just as much as the 300-yard drive.

Former PGA Champion, John Daly, explained, "Any time you win a tournament, you win with your short game. Whether it's chipping or putting, you win tournaments with your short game."

Like many of us, you may have a tendency to focus primarily on long-range and long-term things like attaining your career goals, getting a new venture started, or reaching your retirement goals. Yes, those things are important.

Yet, it's the little things that matter the most: the *short game* of life. Like a championship golfer approaching the "putting green," experiencing "the A+ Life" requires that we focus on what really matters in life. It's the little things in life that make the biggest impact.

A meaningful conversation with your friend. A date with your spouse. 15 minutes reading the Bible. Taking a walk outside to have a conversation with God. Those are little things that make a big difference in your life.

Yes, the short game of our lives is filled with daily challenges, frustrations, and disappointments. Craig Stadler said, "Why am I using a new putter? Because the last one didn't float too well." Sometimes we get tempted to abandon our efforts to focus on the little things in life, often because we usually don't see or feel the immediate results of doing the little things right.

Arnold Palmer said, "Putting is a fascinating, aggravating, wonderful, terrible and most incomprehensible part of the game of golf." This is also the case in the *short game* of our lives. The *short game* is the area of our lives where we find, over time, our deepest fulfillment and satisfaction in life. Yet, in the short term, it can sometimes seem futile, fruitless, and boring.

As I taught adult Sunday School classes for several years, I would look out on the classes and see the ladies paying attention and often taking notes. The men, however, were bored and disengaged. I imagine they were thinking about anything but what I was teaching on.

"What football games are on today?"

"Am I going to meet my sales quota this month?"

"How am I going to get my kids through college?"

"How am I going to make my tee time this afternoon and not make the wife mad?"

My heart went out to these men. They were so lost and missing it. I wanted to cry out to them, "There's more!"

But they weren't listening.

These couples represent the vast majority of people I encounter: good people. Very good people. They are good church members as well. But they are busy and distracted. And no one in their church is telling them they are missing it.

What are they missing? The essential gospel message. It's not about being a good church person, a "Churchian." It's about surrendering to Jesus as your Savior, then surrendering in all of the little things that make up our lives: the *short game*.

This book consists of weekly devotionals written to you to impact your day-to-day living. High theology is not our goal. But life transformation is. I want you to see Jesus in your daily life, and to see clearly that you live in a God-Saturated world. If you do, your life will change, and the Lord will transform you. You will discover "the A+ Life" that Jesus promised when he said, "I have come so they may have life, and life to the full" (John 10:10).

As in the weekly golf tournaments, *The Putting Green Devotional* is divided into four "rounds" of 18 "holes." Each round focuses on helping you in a particular area of your relationship with God and others.

The first "round" is dedicated to helping you grow in the area of your "Priorities," encouraging you to seek God first in everything you do.

Round Two focuses on God's "Grace," the power to help you experience "Life that is truly Life."

The third round will guide you through 18 challenging "holes" on the topic of "Humility," the key to blessed living.

Round Four is dedicated to helping you strengthen your personal "Integrity," the wholeness of character that allows you to honor God in every aspect of your life.

Jack Nicklaus said, "No matter your scoring goals, you can attain them faster by improving your putting." Most of us want to do something great with our lives over the long term. True significance in life happens in the *short game*, the little things that create a life of greatness.

Round 1

Priorities

"Putting is like wisdom – partly a natural gift and partly an accumulation of experience."
-Arnold Palmer, World Golf Hall of Famer

Hole 1

"Good" Distractions

"The seed that fell among thorns stands for those who hear, but as they go on their way they are choked by life's worries, riches and pleasures…"
Luke 8:14

Your "Yes" is so often to something good but nowhere near the best. And your "No," unintentionally but unavoidably, is often to that which is the best. Being distracted by good opportunities will cause you to miss the very best. And Jesus tells story after story about distractions causing us to miss him and his Kingdom.

The third soil in the parable of the four soils is a prime example: "The seed that fell among thorns stands for those who hear, but as they go on their way they are choked by life's worries, riches and pleasures" (Luke 8:14).

So, I ask you to sit down for a moment—can you?—and write down the absolute most important things to you. Ideally, time with your Lord, your spouse, and your children will be at the top, followed perhaps by exercise, rest, relaxation, sleep, and walks… dare I say, even naps?

Take your calendar, planner, or an index card and schedule them in each week as immovable, unchangeable priorities.

Now, with your best priorities fixed in place, consider all future opportunities and invitations as potential enemies to the best.

The next time you are approached about serving on a committee, chairing a board, or signing your child up for yet another activity, you respond, "I'll have to weigh this against my 'best' priorities, and then I'll have to determine what I'd have to say no to."

Your old way of responding is to mindlessly say "yes" without thinking about the consequences of saying "no" to the best.

But now, because you've already scheduled in your exercise, a walk with your spouse, play time with your daughter, or personal time with the Lord, you examine your schedule for openings, first. First!

If you decide this new opportunity or invitation is important enough to say no to something you've already committed to as part of the best, what then will you say "no" to? Make no mistake, you now will have to say "no" to something.

No openings? "No, I couldn't possibly do it" is the reply.

Saying "no" to yourself and your Body-Mind-Spirit needs is just as damaging, if not more so.

Jesus warns us over and over that it will be the good distractions that cause us to miss him and his Kingdom.

Don't be distracted by "good things" and miss his best.

Hole 2

Self-Seeking or Seeking First?

*"But seek first his kingdom and his righteousness,
and all these things will be given to you as well."*
Matthew 6:33

As with my computer's default setting, I wake up each day with a default setting set for, "What does Sam need to be happy today?" If I don't reset that default setting, self-seeking will be the order of the day.

What, or who, do you seek—*first* and foremost—throughout each day?

Is Jesus out of touch to advocate that we should seek Him first? Come on, Jesus... are you expecting me to become a monk? I have to work. I have responsibilities that *demand* my focus. Surely, only the ministry-type people can be expected to seek You first. The rest of us live in the real world.

The real question each of us wants to ask, objectively and honestly, is this: "Is God big enough and *involved* enough for me to truly seek Him first as my top priority in life?"

If He is, then what Jesus is saying can be embraced, knowing that the details will be sorted out as we move through life with Him. If he is not, then Jesus is just a nice prophet, a warm and fuzzy Oprah type. Someone we can enjoy in church, but when the real-life issues surface, we have to get serious and self-seek first, of course.

What does seeking Him first look like? First, it does *not* look like staying in a closet, praying, and expecting God to provide. Only a fool would approach life that way, and he will suffer for it.

But it does look like this: beginning each day with a private time with God. Reading scripture, slowly, and absorbing God's words. Quietly praying and listening. Seeking His pleasure throughout the day, His guidance, and His presence...getting to know Him. It means wanting His will to prevail in your life. I know this may sound radical. Though, we can bring Jesus into our daily schedule, spend time with Him, and still be prudent, proactive, and even aggressive in our work.

We've seen men and women scale back their white-knuckling approach to business, place Jesus as their priority, and actually experience more success. And yes, even make more money.

Jesus also assures us that we can seek the good for others as well, and He will take care of us. It's the familiar Golden Rule: "So in everything, do to others what you would have them do to you, for this sums up the Law and the Prophets" (Matt. 7:7). So, I can actually seek your best over my self-seeking, and God has my back on that, too? Now, that's counter-intuitive! But, what a relational paradise.

Seeking Him first is what we are created to do. Rewards or not, He is worthy of our rapt attention, our heart-felt pursuit.

Hole 3

Stop & Think!

"What good will it be for a man if he gains the whole world,
yet forfeits his soul? Or what can a man give in exchange for his soul?"
Matthew 16:26

Without stopping daily to think about what's really important to you, three *decades* from now, you'll still be... you.

Friedrich Nietzsche made this observation: "The most common form of human stupidity is forgetting what one is trying to do." That one drilled right through me.

I've watched basketball games where the star player goes twenty minutes without even touching the ball. I've watched businessmen develop a core business, make a lot of money, and then start delving into other "investments" where they lose much of what they had gained. I've observed companies grow and gain market share, diversify into other products, and ultimately go bankrupt.

How did these things happen? They forgot what they were trying to do.

I've watched fathers lose their way, focusing on *their* world and forgetting they are fathers: the most important person in their children's lives! Their children suffer terribly from these "forgetful" dads, dads blinded by their "me-cataracts." They have lost vision of what they should be trying to do: be fathers! "The most common form of human stupidity is forgetting what one is trying to do."

You see, we mistakenly think in terms of exchanging as if our time and involvement is a product to be negotiated. "I know she wants me to be at her track meet, cheerleading event, and dance recital, but... I'll make it up to her."

No, you won't. You'll not be able exchange this time for a future time. You have forfeited this opportunity to show her just how incredibly important she is to you. This is true with your wives, your husbands,

7

children, parents, and... your Lord. Stop and think: What are you trying to accomplish in life?

Regarding your family, are you just getting through the day, giving it a minimum effort? That's a D- life. Or, are you intently focused on playing a meaningful role as more than just a provider... a promoter? A promoter puts together, holds together, encourages, and engages... promotes the best for those for whom he or she is responsible. A promoter maximizes his or her time with a focus on maximizing everyone else's.

Minimum effort in your relationship with God is to merely focus on church attendance and church activity. Maximum effort is to say, "I want to know Him intimately and I'll invest my time to do so."

Is where you're going where you want to be when you get there? With your family, as well as with your God, there is no exchanging today for later. It's strictly a forfeiture. Stop and think, please! It's too important not to.

Hole 4

Finding Life

"In this way they will lay up treasure for themselves as a firm foundation for the coming age, so that they may take hold of the life that is truly life."
1 Timothy 6:19

We are all living out a process in this life. Even as the process runs its course across our lives, it is taking place moment by moment, decision by decision… in the present.

This process is not happening in the past, so it's useless to dwell on…

"Why did that happen to me?"

"I can't believe they did that to me."

Nor is this process happening in the future…

"What if…?"

"How will I…?

"If only…"

"One day, I'll…"

This process is being guided by our minds and our hearts. What we believe is what we'll do, and what we treasure is what we'll pursue.

If I think the *Good Life* is about things, my image, how I compare to others, and storing up treasures here on earth—what are driven predominantly by what others think—then I will pursue such things. That pursuit will often be to the detriment of me, my family, and others around me.

The Good Life can encompass any of those things, yes, but as *servants*… not *masters*. If I can embrace a higher consciousness of what Jesus promoted as the real Good Life, then I might find the Life that is truly life. One is a rental, the other… an investment.

Hole 5

Excuse Me

"The seed that fell among thorns stands for those who hear,
but as they go on their way they are choked by life's worries,
riches and pleasures, and they do not mature."
Luke 8:14

Lately, I've been thinking a lot about what I spend much of my time thinking about—and it isn't pretty. My mind is like a pinball machine: bouncing around with no apparent pattern. I am loathe to admit that much of what occupies my thoughts is either self-centered or negative. It's either all about me, or it's all about them: that person who aggravated me or isn't doing what I want.

If God is God, maybe *He* should occupy a larger place in my thoughts. I mean, if He is who most of us *say* He is, is there any excuse for being so mindless when it comes to thinking about Him?

What a ridiculous and—to be blunt—pathetic commentary on our current state of mind. Can we really be that disconnected from what's truly important? If God is God, I think it's appropriate that I allot Him a bigger slot in my thoughts, maybe bring Him closer into my mental orbit. For many of us, as far as our thought patterns go, God is like Pluto: so small and far out of our central orbit that He's even lost planet status!

Satan's best weapon might be distraction: keeping us busy and running stream-of-consciousness thoughts through our minds that are focused on anything but God. In C.S. Lewis' *The Screwtape Letters*, a senior demon in Satan's army is corresponding with a junior demon about the younger demon's new human project. The younger demon's job is to keep the human away from God:

"…you will find that anything or nothing is sufficient to attract his wandering attention. You can make him waste his time not only in conversations with people whom he likes, but also in conversations with those he cares nothing about; on subjects that bore him… so that at last he may say… on his arrival down here, 'I now see that I spent most of my life doing neither what I ought nor what I liked.'"

Ouch. That feels familiar.

The only rational approach to life, if God is God, is to constantly and consistently bring Him into our daily thoughts… to reflect on God's mercy and goodness… to thank Jesus throughout the day for, well, for being Jesus.

If we spent a little more time pondering about His grace, His love, His power, and His majesty—not just while sitting in church—our lives would more naturally fold into the harmony of His gravity field.

Hole 6

It Can't Mean That!

*"We did not follow cleverly invented stories when we told you about
the power and coming of our Lord Jesus Christ,
but we were eyewitnesses of his majesty."*
2 Peter 1:16

Mark Twain liked to say, "It's not the parts of the Bible that I don't understand that bother me; it's the parts that I do understand!"

What about you? Aren't there parts of the Bible that you'd prefer to ignore? Sometimes, if we can't find it in ourselves to ignore those parts, we just rationalize them away. For example: "It no longer applies to me at this time in history… certainly I'm not to be expected to take it at face value."

In a court of law, the most powerful evidence is eyewitness testimony. If you've ever testified, you're very familiar with the cry, "Hearsay your honor! Not admissible." Consider the writers of the New Testament. The disciples—Matthew, John, and Peter—were eyewitnesses. Jesus' little brothers, James and Jude, were also eyewitnesses. Luke assures us that he was an eyewitness companion with Paul and that he interviewed eyewitnesses.

Now, this is really cool. Irenaeus—Bishop of Lyons in AD 180, who was a student of Polycarp, Bishop of Smyrna (who had been a Christian for 86 years and was a disciple of John the Apostle)—wrote:

"Matthew published his gospel among the Hebrews (i.e. Jews) in their own tongue, when Peter and Paul were preaching the gospel in Rome and founding the church there. After their departure (i.e. death, which strong tradition places at the time of the Neronian persecution in 64), Mark, the disciple and interpreter of Peter, himself handed down to us the substance of Peter's preaching. Luke, the follower of Paul, set down in a book the gospel preached by his teacher. Then John, the disciple of the Lord, who also leaned on his breast (see John 13:25 and 21:20), himself produced his gospel, while he was living at Ephesus in Asia."

I find these men's testimony compelling, especially when I consider their motives. They received no book deals or talk show circuit. Instead, they were whipped, beaten, ostracized, and killed… violently.

So, I encourage you to start making a daily practice of reading this Bible. Start at John's gospel. Read slowly—we're not in a hurry. If it feels dry, awkward, or even boring at first, ask God to meet you in His Word. He will help you to hear His voice. Make God's Word the top priority in your life.

Hole 7

My Trust Factor

"I am the light of the world. Whoever follows me will never walk in darkness,
but will have the light of life."
John 8:12

I will never find this Life that is truly life if I don't do a little self-reliance research into where I place my trust, in whom I place my trust, and on what my trust is based.

Most of us trust in our treasures. They are called treasures because we *treasure* them; we value them; they give us value. We lean on them; we depend on them; we trust in them to give us a sense of worth. To find and stay in the Good Life, we must loosen our grip on our treasures.

I had an ex-marine coach who liked to squeeze my hand so tightly when we shook hands that it would bring tears to my eyes. He would grin and say, "Be careful boy not to grab something that won't let you go."

Loosen your grip on what you treasure. Your treasures will determine your legacy, what you stood for. Moment by moment, decision by decision, you are forming your legacy. You are painting your own self-portrait day each day. These actions and decisions may not seem monumental at the time—in the present—they will determine who you are and what you stood for.

Is what you will have stood for eternally significant or eternally insignificant?

Hole 8

Surprises

"Not everyone who says to me, 'Lord, Lord,' will enter the kingdom of heaven, but only he who does the will of my Father who is in heaven. Many will say to me on that day, 'Lord, Lord, did we not prophesy in your name, and in your name drive out demons and perform many miracles?' Then I will tell them plainly, 'I never knew you. Away from me, you evildoers!'"
Matthew 7:21-23

I once showed up at a party completely underdressed. I mean, I had clothes on for crying out loud, but alongside everyone else's suits, my polo shirt cut me down from a self-confident 6'-1" to an antsy 4'-3".

Ever experienced something similar? An unpleasant surprise? That pop quiz you weren't ready for? A social or business situation that caught you unprepared?

Let's take a look at some of the surprises about which Jesus seemed compelled to warn us. If we read the Gospels with an awareness of this aspect of Jesus' teachings, we will see His warnings over and over—and over. It's as if He's saying:

> "Folks, you really don't have a clue about what's waiting on the other side, nor about what's really important. You seem to have this disconnect between where you are headed, and where you *say* to want to be."

We might intend to end up in Heaven, we might intend to live Godly lives, lives that please God and *count* for what's really important, but if we are operating on the wrong information, or moving in the wrong direction, well, we may be surprised. And what an unpleasant surprise that could be.

Jesus has warned us that many people will show up on Judgment Day—yes, our sweet, loving, warm, and fuzzy Jesus—and start listing their church and civic activities as proof that they've earned their way into heaven. He practically shouts His warning to us: "Then, I will tell them plainly, 'I never knew you. Away from me, you evildoers" (Matt. 7:23).

Jesus also warns, "Do not work for food that spoils, but for food that endures to eternal life, which the Son of Man will give you" (John 6:27). The warning here is to not spend your life on things that have no eternal value, but instead, to invest your life in what does.

As Andy Stanley says, "Direction determines Destination— direction, *not intent*, determines your destination." Is where you're going where you want to be when you get there?

Hole 9

Preoccupied!

"Be careful, or your hearts will be weighed down with dissipation,
drunkenness and the anxieties of life, and that day
will close on you unexpectedly like a trap."
Luke 21:34

I'm thirteen, we're behind by one run, and I'm on first base. Because I was a superior athlete... I'm leading off the base ready to steal second. Cute Barbara Shenkel walks up to the fence. I'm so cool, so I smile, and the next thing I know I'm the goat in the dugout. Picked off! A fool.

This was neither the first nor the last time I missed out because I was preoccupied. Distracted. My attention diverted. After a few days, when Dad let me sleep in the house again, I got over the humiliation and disappointment.

A few days. Not such a big deal. But what if I was distracted, preoccupied with my own little world, and I missed something that I regretted for eternity?

The Master Teacher, the one who wants you and me to experience the best life possible, both here and in Heaven, could see that many of us would fall victim to distractions and preoccupation with, well, you name it.

Of course, your distractions might be neither frivolous nor wasteful. Yours may be all about serious stuff or even good stuff: work, committees, boards, tennis leagues, your children's 500 activities. Though, maybe the result is still the same. You're preoccupied. You're missing the essence of the spiritual life: "Now this is eternal life: that they may know you, the only true God, and Jesus Christ, whom you have sent" (John 17:3).

Our sweet, loving Jesus almost sounds like He's threatening us, with this "and that day will close on you unexpectedly like a trap" talk. Yet, if He's right—and we know He is—then we might just need to be threatened, or at a minimum, doused with some cold water reality. Actually,

Jesus is simply warning us from His heart that many of us are, sometimes with the best of intentions, going in the wrong direction.

I challenge you to look inside yourself. Run an *all systems check* on your life, your heart, and your comfort level with your current focus on what's really important.

Hole 10

Superman

"I pray also that the eyes of your heart may be enlightened in order that you may know the hope to which he has called you, the riches of his glorious inheritance in the saints, and his incomparably great power for us who believe."
Ephesians 1:18-19

Are you old enough to remember when Christopher Reeve's first *Superman* movie came out back in 1978? A group of us knuckleheads went to see the movie and were blown away by the special effects. At one point, Superman is flying, and he drops his left shoulder and eases off to the left in this intercontinental super swoop. It was so cool.

One Halloween, I dressed up as Superman. Boy! Was I on top of the world! Ready to conquer all the bad guys... until that flimsy band on my mask broke about five minutes into the night. And then, the cape wouldn't stay on, much less flow behind me as I acted like I was flying by running at breakneck speed.

Which of Superman's powers would you most like to have? Isn't it fun to think about? The ability to fly? Super strength? Super hearing? X-ray vision? Reading minds? When I was younger, I would have automatically said *flying*. No doubt! Soaring around in the sky! How great would that be? Of course, having super strength would have been really cool with the girls.

As I season through life, I recognize the extraordinary value of being able to see things clearly and accurately. Today, my superpower of choice would be x-ray vision... in the sense of discernment, clarity, and spiritual vision.

Do you think you can see things clearly? Can you see things the way they really are? Do you think you see the world more accurately than most people? I used to think so. I had it all figured out. Now, though, I'm not so self-assured. What I'm now realizing is my vision is clouded. It's clouded with prejudice, pre-conceived notions, and self-serving inclinations. It's clouded mostly by the fact that I am just not that smart.

19

Though, the more I seek to see through the Light of Jesus' perspective on life, the more I begin to truly *see*. Jesus tried to tell me that a long time ago: "I am the light of the world. Whoever follows me will never walk in darkness, but will have the light of life" (John 8:12).

I don't want to wander around in the darkness anymore. I don't want to trust my limited vision, my self-deluded heart. So, I look to Jesus. Like Bartimaeus, I simply say, "Rabbi, I want to see."

In turn, Jesus says to me, "Whoever has my commands and obeys them, he is the one who loves me. He who loves me will be loved by my Father, and I too will love him and show myself to him" (John 14:21).

What a promise! If we follow Jesus, seek Him as our Lord and Leader, we'll be able to see Him… truly *see* Him.

Hole 11

New Beginnings

"Let us fix our eyes on Jesus, the author and perfecter of our faith."
Hebrews 12:2

Have you been meaning to cut back on your smoking, drinking, eating, cussing, arguing, gossiping, lusting, judging… closing that dreary old chapter and starting a new one, today. You can finally do it!

Have you been lazy and out of shape? Not getting enough sleep? Your life is way too busy, filled with "good" activities? Edit that part of the story and write this in: "Saying *yes* to something always means you'll have to say *no* to something else." So often, we end up saying *no* to things that are most important to us. Today, write these priorities back into your story and cut out what is *good* but not the *best*.

Have you been carrying around that bitterness inside for far too long. You know it, too. You say, "But they were wrong to hurt me; what they did was so bad!" I know, and they probably were wrong, but get out your eraser today and rub out that episode. Breathe the fresh air of forgiveness, and *you* write a new ending to what *they* did.

Have you known that God has more for you than you've been experiencing with him. You've seen it in other people. Okay, it makes you nervous to think about what a deeper pursuit of Jesus might involve. Drop that obstinate stiff-arm and begin a new chapter of a full-on embrace of a passionate pursuit of Jesus.

Have you been meaning to read your Bible more—or, at least, some—but you say, "Gosh, it's so busy around my house in the morning." Yet, we know that what's important to us gets done, and what's not, well, it doesn't. This coming year, close that lazy chapter and write a new story about your desire to know your Creator better.

Paul writes, "Brothers . . . one thing I do: Forgetting what is behind and straining toward what is ahead, I press on toward the goal to win the prize for which God has called me heavenward in Christ Jesus" (Phil. 3:13-14).

21

Jesus is standing at the door of your life saying, "Is where you're going where you want to be when you get there? Come, start a new beginning with me today, and let's enjoy the ending together."

Today, you can start living in the direction of where you want to be when you get there. No more procrastination. No more looking back. No more mediocrity. No more, "I'll get to that later." Allow God to help you change your course today! Even your "B" life pales to the "A+" life Jesus has for you.

Jesus is the real Author, and we are just dime-store novelists, penning shallow romance novels without him. Yet, Jesus lovingly invites us to be the editor of our own life story. Fix your eyes on the Author, and take out your pen, today! As Paul Harvey said, what will "The Rest of the Story" be in your life?

Hole 12

I Want

"Ask and it will be given to you; seek and you will find; knock and the door will be opened to you . . . Here I am! I stand at the door and knock."
Matthew 7:7; Revelation 3:20

What do you want? Have you stopped to examine this question... really examine? What do I really want? What is most important for me to possess, to find, to know?

Need some help? Try this: "If you look at what you've ended up with, then you'll know what you've actually been seeking."

If you are too busy, stressed by all that comes your way each day then, apparently, that's what you wanted.

Are you overweight or out of shape? Then...

Are you drowning in possessions that actually possess you? Then...

Is your marriage stale, or worse? Then...

If your religion is not the full, abundant life Jesus promised... apparently, you don't want it to be.

Many of us are just like plankton, drifting along the currents of this vapid culture, absorbing whatever flows at us. We don't know what we want. Or, we've never actually thought deeply about it. So, we accept... whatever.

Jesus had this penetrating way of asking whomever he encountered, "What do you want me to do for you?" He asked the crippled man, "Do you want to get well?" I can hear the inflection in Jesus' voice: "Do you really *want* to be healed, or do you just want a little help today with your list of troubles?"

What most of us want from Jesus is a taxi ride: "Get me out of this mess; solve this problem; give me this; fix him or change her." When the problem is fixed, we step out of the taxi, thank God for his help, and say, "Don't go too far. I'll call you when I need you next." Oh my.

Before we can chart a course for the A+ life Jesus promised, we must answer the question, "What do I truly want?"

A few years ago, I was fond of telling friends I wanted to learn to play the piano. After being challenged to do something about it, I bought a piano and started lessons. After a year of misery, I realized I really didn't want to *learn* to play, I just wanted to be able to *play*... magically... with no real work on my part.

So, if you made any New Year's resolutions, I'd challenge you to stop and first determine if you really want those resolutions, or do you just wish for them?

Hole 13

My Wants, His Wants

"Then you will call upon me and come and pray to me, and I will listen to you.
You will seek me and find me when you seek me with all your heart."
Jeremiah 29:13

Again, I ask, what is it you want? Is there even a remote part of you that truly wants what God wants for you? Is this only true if it lines up with your list of wants? Is your list of *wants* so pathetic and shallow that it consists primarily of self-centered desires like, "I want her to change. I want him to stop. I want them to start. If I could only have a little more money, clothes, house, sex, affection, fun, variety, thrills, and control... just a *little* more and I'll be happy." Really?

First and foremost, I want to actually *want*. Yes, before any progress can be made I must first actually want to want!

Second, I want God to help me transform my wants to His wants.

Third and most important, the want that will transform everything about me: "I want to know Christ and the power of his resurrection... For to know him is to love him" (Phil. 3:10). A life guided by love for Jesus... a life energized by, motivated by, and powered by love for God the Father is truly the only A+ life.

Reflect, think, and pray deeply about what you really want in life. Then, with Jesus guiding the way, go out and get it!

Do you know Jesus? Really know him? I have many friends, some I know better than others and some I know more *about* than others. Though, the air is pretty thin with those about whom I can truly say, "I know him inside and out. I know how she thinks. I know what moves him. I sense what she senses. I feel what he feels."

Imagine if you could say this about Jesus? Now, that would be an adventure. Imagine the freedom, confidence, clarity, and peace that would envelop you if you were on an intimate, first-name, even nick-name, basis with Jesus. It is rarified air, to be sure. The absolute promise is this: you can, if you want.

Do you want it? If you do, you can have it. But, maybe you don't really want it. You're busy... a lot on the plate. You can get to this later.

Jesus prefaced many of his statements with, "If you..." In perfect keeping with his deep understanding of human nature, Jesus is again reinforcing, "If you truly want something from me, then you will do what it takes to get it." In God's Kingdom, "doing what it takes to get it" does not look like the usual gritting of teeth or New Year's resolution to *do more*. It looks like wanting... wanting it so much we are seeking it with all our heart, then, asking for help. We will only do this when we know we need help. When we ask for and want real movement, real growth... I'd call it transformation.

Do you seek to be transformed or just polished up?

God has promised that if we really want to find him, we will. All we have to do is really want it. The first step is that simple.

Hole 14

Press On

"For the Son of Man is going to come in his Father's glory with his angels,
and then he will reward each person according to what he has done."
Matthew 16:27

There is a reward system in heaven. The Bible is saturated with encouragements and warnings about this reward system. What you do *here* in this life with your time and your money also matters *there*, in Heaven. We do not earn salvation, nor do we earn more of God's love or affection. That's important to understand. However, we do earn rewards.

God will not love you more or even like you more. His love is complete. Though, it matters to him what you do, how you live, and where your heart is. It matters so much he makes it clear he is noticing and keeping an account. Precisely because he loves you so much, he wants to welcome you with, "Well done, good and faithful servant! You have been faithful with a few things; I will put you in charge of many things. Come and share your master's happiness!" (Matt. 25:23).

Think of it this way. When you sense the Holy Spirit prompting you to help more, to give more, to write that check, or to make that phone call—whatever the conviction is—do not think, "If I do this, I'll get a reward." No, the heart tuned into God instead thinks, "This matters to my Heavenly Father."

Yes, I will to listen to this conviction in my heart. I want to go, to help, and to give because he has come, helped, and given so much. You see, I want to live the A+ Life Jesus wants for me. I have seen it. I have stepped into it. I have experienced the rewards with its warmth, peace, joy, contentment, and the incredibly positive energy. Yes, I have from time to time let it slip away as I turned back towards the kingdom of Sam, away from the only true King and his Kingdom.

Though, I am not discouraged. I press on. The journey is before me, not behind me. I have not fully obtained this A+ Life yet, but I am on the path. Each day, I ask the Holy Spirit to assist me and energize me.

Hole 15

Saying "Yes" to the Right Things

*"Be careful not to do your 'acts of righteousness' before men, to be seen by them. If you
do, you will have no reward from your Father in heaven."*
Matthew 6:1

Vince Lombardi, one of the greatest pro football coaches of all time, told his players, "If you will put God first, then your families, and then the Green Bay Packers, we will be successful." This is the same coach who said, "Winning isn't everything; it's the only thing!"

Why would this hard-driving and successful coach want his players to put God and their families before his team? Simple. He knew that without the proper priorities, they could be good, but not great... a "B," maybe, but no "A+."

Most of us put our effort and focus first on the areas that our culture requires and rewards. Our energy, creativity, and proactivity are spent on work, community work, and church work. These are where we get our public pats on the back.

At our jobs, no one gets a promotion for being a loving and devoted spouse or parent. In community work, no one gets their picture in the paper for quietly helping the struggling friend or neighbor, or personally assisting that disadvantaged person. In church work, no one gets recognized at church for their personal devotion time at home, or for reading Scripture and praying and spending time alone seeking God.

When we say "Yes" to any of these good things over our families, we are saying, "This is more important to me than you are." Of course, we don't speak those words, but that's what your wife, your husband, your children hear, loud and clear. "You are not as important to me as these other activities." To be blunt, "I get more reward from these activities than I do being with you." Trust me. They hear it, they feel it; they know it. And, it scars them deeply.

Then, there's God. Your Creator, who loves you dearly. He hears it, too. One day, we will each stand before him. "Gosh, God, I was so busy.

There just wasn't time to spend with you. The mornings? Forget it; there was so much to be done. Can't you see that?"

God will reply, "The important things got done. I wasn't as important to you as those other things."

The only logical approach is to decide to purposefully say "Yes" to God first, each day, each morning. Can you squeeze him in for 30 minutes to start the day? Say "Yes" to your family. Say "Yes" to your health and fitness.

Then, you'll be forced to say "No" to many of the dizzying busy calls for your time. You'll say "No" to the numbing busyness of every board, civic organization, children's activity, and church committee.

You have to cheat somewhere, someone, some group. Will it be God? Will it be your family? Will it be your health and fitness? Even if you don't decide, you've decided. Choose wisely and grab for the gusto of that A+ life!

Hole 16

Distracted!

*"It is written: 'Man does not live on bread alone,
but on every word that comes from the mouth of God. "*
Matthew 4:4

Nicodemus was distracted by his entrenched religious traditions when Jesus met him.

The Samaritan woman tried to distract Jesus with stiff-arming questions like "What if?" and "How could?"

Martha was distracted by busyness. Without realizing it, Martha used her busyness to stiff-arm Jesus.

Satan loves busyness, and he revels in our distractions. At every staff meeting, he reminds his minions, "If you can't make them bad, make them busy." Next time you're out in a restaurant or in public, take a look around you. See all the faces buried in their Blackberry's and iPhones. Distractions! I don't have to know you to know you're too busy and far too distracted. Being Mary in a Martha world is challenging. It is so counter-cultural. It's almost impossible.

You know this Martha and Mary story, don't you? (Luke 10) Jesus arrives at Lazarus' house. As Jesus begins teaching, Mary sits to listen at his feet. You can be sure she's not taking notes about theology. She's absorbing *him.* She's worshipping in Spirit and in Truth. Martha is incensed, however, that she is left with all the preparations.

I have no doubt Martha is not really burdened by her busyness. She loves it. It *defines* her. Being busy is how she finds her self-worth. Oh sure, she likes to protest, "Someone's got to do it! If I don't, who will? Preparations must be made. The work of the church must go on!" Jesus would smile, lovingly, but shake his head and say, "The *work* of God is to believe in the one he has sent."

So, as Martha complains about Mary just sitting there listening to Jesus, Jesus lays a penetrating truth on her: "Martha, Martha, you are worried and upset about many things, but only one thing is needed. Mary has chosen what is better, and it will not be taken away from her."

Martha's identity is anchored in her reputation for always being busy, in charge, and the most productive. Since her identity is anchored in anything other than the "only one thing that is needed," she is easily, "worried and upset about many things."

I want you to ask yourself, "What is my identity anchored to?" If it is anchored to anything other than an ever-growing and ever-deepening relationship with Jesus, it will be a loose anchor. And a loose anchor is not an anchor at all, is it?

What about you? Do you find yourself too busy to stop, think, and make sure you're chasing after what's most important? Be still and know that *He* is God!

Hole 17

Focus on Jesus

"Come to me, all you who are weary and burdened, and I will give you rest."
Matthew 11:28

Though Martha found herself "busy" and distracted by the trivial things of this world, Mary had chosen to be still and sit at the feet of Jesus. The Lord said that "Mary has chosen what is better, and it will not be taken away from her." Because of this stillness before the Lord, she had what would never be taken away from her—*him*—and that larger, stronger, quieter life with him.

Do you know any Marys? Probably not many. Aren't they a peaceful joy to be around? I bet you know a lot of Marthas.

Jesus is beckoning, "Come to me. Get away with me and you'll recover your life. I'll show you how to take a real rest. Walk with me and work with me; watch how I do it. Learn the unforced rhythms of grace. Keep company with me and you'll learn to live freely and lightly" (Matt. 11:28-30).

Watching TV, reading the paper, surfing through your iPhone, Crackberry, Facebook… anything is easier than sitting still to read Scripture, sitting quietly with the Lord, or even just sitting quietly.

Each morning when we awake, the day's busyness rushes at us. If we just get out of bed and step straight into it, we don't stand a chance against the push and pull of this culture. This is why having an early-morning, quiet devotional time with the Lord is so vital. Writing 70 years ago in the good old days when life was slower, C.S. Lewis said,

> "The real problem of the Christian life comes where people do not usually look for it. It comes the very moment you wake up each morning. All your wishes and hopes for the day rush at you like wild animals. And the first job each morning consists simply in shoving them all back; in listening to that other voice taking that other point of view, letting that other, larger, stronger, quieter life come flowing in." (Mere Christianity)

We can learn so much from the example that Mary set. It is far better to sit in the presence of God and focus on what's really important. Let's not allow busyness to cause us to miss our defining moments before God as Martha did when she had the chance.

Hole 18

One Day

"What good will it be for someone to gain the whole world, yet forfeit their soul?
Or what can anyone give in exchange for their soul?"
Matthew 16:26

Quick, picture the great life you envision when you think about the life you hope to have *one day*. (Really, take a moment. Mine has horses in the future pasture behind my future farm house with a young filly kicking around.) Don't all of us have this idea of "one day" which we think about when our minds are floating off into daydreams? It's the day when we finally have the desires of our hearts. Finally. One day.

Without knowing you, I know a few things about your "one day" image: there is no stress. Money is secure and there's a little (or a lot) more than you actually need. There is unconditional love, both romantic love and family love. There is good health so you can go and do what you want.

Again, without knowing you, I can predict what is *not* prevalent in your daydream: your spiritual life. Am I wrong? Oh, I'm not saying you don't care about it; I'm just saying it's not a leading component when you think about that "one day."

How many of you immediately thought, "And I'll be in a deeper, more intimate, and more rewarding relationship with Jesus?" Or, "I'll be so close to God, I'll sense his will for me step by step as I go about my daily life? And I'll be living with such power from the Holy Spirit that his energy, clarity, and creativity will overflow through me into the lives of those around me."

This would be an unusual daydream, wouldn't you agree? I would think it was a tad odd, to be honest. I don't daydream that way, and I'm in the business! But, I want to. And I have started to visualize this. Will you join me? Because "one day" is fast approaching, my friends.

Jesus spoke many times about the regret people will experience as they reach their "one day" and realize it's not what they wanted or expected, or—and don't miss this—*intended* it to be. Jesus wants you to be intentional about your journey.

Regret at having "missed it" is an overarching theme in Jesus' teachings, and his parables echo this constant drumbeat. Jesus often concludes his parables with, "And there will be wailing and crying out and gnashing of teeth." I'm not sure what gnashing of teeth is, but I know I don't want to be doing it. When Jesus says, "For whoever wants to save his life will lose it, but whoever loses his life for me will find it. What good will it be for a man if he gains the whole world, yet forfeits his soul?" (Matthew 16). He is imploring us to periodically check our path and ask this important question to re-center our direction.

I'll leave you with this: we are all on the journey towards 'there.' Your Heavenly Father wants you to experience all the riches of his Kingdom every day in this life and in the next life. We must ask ourselves honestly, "Am I presently heading in that A+ direction?"

Round 2

Grace

"I don't fear death, but I sure don't like those three-footers for par."
-Chi Chi Rodriguez

Hole 1

Amazing Grace

*"Let the groans of the prisoners come before you;
according to your great power, preserve those doomed to die!"*
Psalm 79:11

Do you often think about God's grace? It is truly an amazing thing to ponder. Grace is getting what you do not deserve. Grace is God's unmerited favor.

Did you know Jesus never uttered the word grace—not once? He just lived it and died for it. For you. So you could experience it. You. Flawed, prideful, judgmental, self-absorbed, and selfish you. You are loved, tenderly and adoringly, by God Almighty, El Shaddai, Creator of the universe. Now, that is amazing.

The writers of the New Testament spoke a lot about grace. Their gratitude was overwhelming and overflowing. It's as if they felt like Jesus had freed them from prison.

If you have surrendered your life to Jesus, you are saved. This means Jesus plucked you out of a prison with a death sentence hanging over your head, took your blame, absorbed your shame, and reconciled you with God. Amazing.

Recently, I was talking with a friend who had actually been to prison. We were talking about how much she has grown spiritually and how much Jesus has transformed her heart. You see, my friend had gotten caught up in a lifestyle that was not "walking in the Light." One thing led to another, and she was sentenced to seven years in prison. She is from a nice family and had a nice family of her own. (Feel free to cast the first stone…)

I asked her if she ever allowed herself to think about what it was like in prison, or did she have to block that completely from her mind? She said, "Oh no, I think about it all the time. And this may surprise you, but, I think about how grateful I am—all the time."

Perplexed, I asked, "Grateful that you're out, and free?"

She replied, "Well, yes, of course. But, I'm also grateful for going to prison. You see, Sam, I was in a different kind of prison before I went to prison." Oh my.

As you are reading this, some of you are lighting up and joining her with a resounding, "Yes, me too! I know just what you mean." Others of you are cynical and thinking, "Oh, another jailhouse conversion." Some of you are thinking, "Well, I'm not perfect, but in prison? Oh, come on, that's for you 'gutter to glory' types."

Which, can only mean… you still are… in prison.

The Apostle Paul joins my friend with overflowing gratitude for being rescued from his own prison: "For he has rescued us from the dominion of darkness and brought us into the kingdom of the Son he loves, in whom we have redemption, the forgiveness of sins" (Col. 1:13-14).

Rescued. Redeemed. The Kingdom of Light. Forgiven. Grace. Amazing.

Hole 2

Pretty Good, but Good Enough?

"Because by one sacrifice he has made perfect forever
those who are being made holy."
Hebrews 10:14

In *Saving Private Ryan,* Captain Miller leads a group of Army Rangers into German-occupied France to rescue a young Private Ryan, whose three brothers were killed during D-Day. At the end of the story, with the dead and wounded all around, Captain Miller pulls young Ryan close and says, "Earn this. Earn it." He was saying, "Don't let these men die in vain. Earn their sacrifice by living a good life."

The scene then morphs to a visibly shaken Ryan as an older man, looking at Captain Miller's grave and saying, "I've never forgotten what you said that day. I tried to live my life the best I could. I hope it was enough." Ryan's wife approaches, and he turns to her, lips quivering and pleads, "I *did* live a good life, didn't I? *Didn't* I?"

Oh my.

It makes my heart hurt to think about that kind of angst. What will be the answer for each of us? And how can we avoid getting to that point in life distressed, filled with trepidation, because we don't know the answer?

"I'll work harder. I'll redouble my efforts *to do* better. I'll up my commitment level. I'll be sure to do the things that will qualify me. I'll *be* better!"

How will we know if it's good enough? And who is the authority? Private Ryan's wife assured him he had indeed lived a good life. But she's sort of like the Women's Gymnastics judges at the Olympics. I wouldn't bet my life on it.

I don't want to get to that point in my life and be troubled, left to wonder if I've done okay... left to *hope* that it was enough. So how can we know? What can we do?

When I place my trust in Jesus and surrender to Him daily, He lifts me from my earthly grade of C+ at best, to a perfect score.

I can dismiss any worries about the good enough performance thing. Sure, I'll still do my part by focusing on His teaching as the way, but my pace will be much more relaxed. I'm no longer stressing and striving. I'm following… His lead.

Hole 3

Insanity or Transformation?

"Then you will call upon me and come and pray to me, and I will listen to you.
You will seek me and find me when you seek me with all your heart."
Jeremiah 29:12-13

The top ten resolutions each New Year start with these: lose weight, pay down debt, quit smoking, exercise more, get organized, and help others. We usually want to change and improve, so we start with things we are going to *do*. We determine to work our way into change.

If you made a list of spiritual resolutions for the New Year—by the way, I found no articles about spiritual New Year's resolutions—what would you include? Pray more? Read the Bible more? Go to church more? Give more money? Attend that Bible Study you *keep meaning* to attend?

All of these are good, but they are yet again about *doing*.

I typically start each January reading Jesus' "Sermon on the Mount" (Matthew 5-7). This year, as I read Jesus' words on *judging*—"Don't do it"—I was convicted to my core. I was like a frog gigged and flopping around on the floor, trying to pull the skewer out of my heart, knowing what an utter wretch I am about judging people. So, I determined to change, to not judge, to *do* better this year.

Later that day, I was pulling into the crowded parking lot of my gym—crowded due to all the *slugs* who resolved to exercise more (see, there I go again)—and I saw a space right at the front with a car about to pull out. So, I waited and 20 minutes later (actually, it was only about one minute), they finally backed out. I thought to myself, "What a dumb knucklehead."

I couldn't even *do* better for one afternoon!

The colloquial definition of *insanity* is, "Doing the same thing over and over and expecting a different result." Based on that, I've been insane most of my life.

Here's the deal. When we determine to *do* better, we will have limited success if any at all. But when we first look to the Lord to change us

43

from the inside out, when we enlist the power of God's Holy Spirit, we stand to see real and lasting change.

Actually, we are not so much changed as we are *transformed*.

Try to grit your teeth and do better? Good luck. Insist on disciplining your way to change? Well, some of you, a few, are indeed very strong in the self-discipline area, so you'll work your way to a grade of B minus—more likely, a C plus.

Please know that I'm all for doing better, self-discipline, and making a plan of action. These have a very real place in our spiritual journey. They just cannot be the lead horse.

Get to know your heavenly Father and His Son, Jesus.

Ask God to move in you. Seek His presence in your life. Seek a personal, one-on-one interaction with Jesus—not a group hug.

Hole 4

Rhythm

"Come to me, all you who are weary and burdened, and I will give you rest. Take my yoke upon you and learn from me, for I am gentle and humble in heart, and you will find rest for your souls. For my yoke is easy and my burden is light."
Matthew 11:28-30

We need more *rhythm* in our lives. No, I'm not talking about taking dancing lessons; otherwise, I would already be a lost cause. I want to live with more harmony, to be in sync, and to move through this life with a sense of God's purpose and pleasure.

I love to see a great athlete in a groove or a dancer gliding across the stage. Recently, I saw a star basketball player struggling in a game. He was out of sync, having to work at it with a 6'-5" defender in his face constantly. Then, he hit a long jump shot. His groove was coming back. His motions, once jerky and forced, became fluid and natural. He was in *rhythm,* and his moves appeared *effortless.* The defenders guarding him no longer seemed to be a problem for him. Regardless of what they did, he was now playing his game. He was focused—in a zone. He had found his *rhythm.*

Is that your life? Do you feel a sense of balance and ease? Are you walking and working in harmony with God? Or, are you like most of us, doing well at times but not so much at others. Are your circumstances, like defenders in a basketball game, dictating your moods?

There is a rhythm that can be had in this life, even amongst the jerky and unpredictable circumstances that inevitably roll at us. Like exceptional athletic, musical, and artistic talent, this rhythm cannot be created solely by our own effort. Our New Year's resolutions will take us only so far. We need help.

When we are out of rhythm, we know it. Life is jerky. Our relationships are jerky. Our focus is scattered. Worry, anxiety, impatience, addiction, greed, and lust become our dance partners, and they have the lead. Instead of sensing God's direction and the flow of His Spirit guiding us, we try to take control. If you are trying to *do* religion and trying *really hard*—even with much sincerity—you'll experience this same sense of struggle. It becomes not so much *Good News*; it's more like challenging news, news that requires you to work hard. But truly, the more relationship replaces religion, the smoother the ride. How?

Surrender, seek, and saturate yourself in Jesus. Stop counting your dance steps and find the unforced rhythms of His grace.

Hole 5

He's a Great Dad!

"But the father said to his servants, 'Quick! Bring the best robe and put it on him.
Put a ring on his finger and sandals on his feet. Bring the fattened calf and kill it.
Let's have a feast and celebrate.'"
Luke 15:22-23

What Jesus wants us to see in his Parable of the Prodigal Son is the true nature of our Heavenly Father. "Prodigal" means, "Wastefully or recklessly extravagant... Giving or yielding profusely; lavish... Lavishly abundant." Our God is, indeed, a *prodigal* Father. His love and the outpouring of that love, is recklessly extravagant. His grace and the outpouring of that grace is lavishly abundant. His celebration when one of us turns back to him is wastefully wonderful.

What an extravagant Father! He is undaunted in his love for you and me. We can rebel, insult him, resent his grace, and reject his love, but he will stay on the porch waiting for us to come to our senses and return home.

In the prodigal parable, both sons rebelled. The younger son's rebellion was an in-your-face rebellion. But, so was the older brother. He said, "Look, *you*!" and then proceeded to dress down his dad with a scornful tone. As with these two misguided sons, our Heavenly Father patiently allows our childish diatribes and loves us despite our ignorance. He is not easily offended and—don't miss this—he is *not* controlling. He will allow us to lose our own way, if we insist. But, all the while, he is ready to run across the fields to meet us when we so much as turn back in his direction. What a lavish Father!

Does any of this sound familiar? God is patient, God is kind. God does not envy, he does not boast, he is not proud. God is not rude, he is not self-seeking, he is not easily angered, he keeps no record of wrongs. God does not delight in evil, but rejoices with the truth. God always protects, always trusts, always hopes, and always perseveres. God never fails....us. (1 Cor. 13:4-8, Adapted).

47

God doesn't need us, or our love: he's God Almighty! Yet, like any loving father, he is saddened by our rebellion because he knows the joy of his love we are missing. He laments the richness we are forfeiting. He lovingly waits to embrace us if we will just open the door: "Here I am! I stand at the door and knock. If anyone hears my voice and opens the door, I will come in and eat with him, and he with me" (Rev. 3:20).

"The Lord is not slow in keeping his promise, as some understand slowness. He is patient with you, not wanting anyone to perish, but everyone to come to repentance" (2 Pet. 3:9).

"And I pray that you, being rooted and established in love, may have power, together with all the saints, to grasp how wide and long and high and deep is the love of Christ, and to know this love that surpasses knowledge—that you may be filled to the measure of all the fullness of God" (Eph. 3:17-19). What a great dad!

Hole 6

Diva to Disciple

*"For he chose us in him before the creation of the world to be holy and blameless in his sight. In love he predestined us to be adopted as his sons through Jesus Christ...
in accordance with the riches of God's grace that he
lavished on us with all wisdom and understanding."*
Ephesians 1:4-8

I like that *lavished* part, don't you? And *holy and blameless in his sight?* Adored. Special. Kind of like being a diva—a diva Christian.

What I like most about being a follower of Jesus is that I don't have to do a thing to earn it. In fact, I cannot earn it! *It* being salvation, God's love, and His affection. He loves me and even *likes* me, just as I am. Just... as... you... are. No upgrades, no makeovers, no prettying up... just as we are. Wow.

But, He loves us too much to allow us to stay the way we are.

Uh oh.

I knew it! I knew there was a catch! All this talk about grace being a gift... about grace being the unmerited (unearned) favor of God... and about Jesus saying, "Come to me all you who are weary and burdened and I will give you rest"(Matt. 11:28) ... as in, "Just relax and rest in My love and grace."

But it is true. After moving my residence from the Kingdom of Sam into the Kingdom of God, when Jesus lit up my life with His Holy Spirit, I became lavished with the riches of God's grace. God does indeed see me as holy and blameless. Me... Sam... holy and blameless!

Check this out: "...Because by one sacrifice he has made perfect forever those who are being made holy" (Heb. 10:14).

That's two absolute words: "perfect forever." No wiggle room. There are no degrees of perfect and forever. We are made perfect forever in God's sight through our relationship with His Son.

And yes, He does see us as holy and blameless from that time on. Period. But there is that little matter of *are being made holy*. This phrase indicates that there is a process going on. The great news is that we are privileged to play a role with the God of the universe in our *being made holy.* Now that's going to take some effort on our part.

Before I say another word about *effort,* a seemingly dirty word in Christianese, may I ask you to toss out any preconceived notions of the old bait and switch *catch?* This is not about another list of things to do. I'm not going to suggest activities that will garner more of God's love and affection. This is not about *performance.*

This is about remaining in the Father's lap of lavish luxury of grace and love while growing in and through that lavish grace and love to be more and more Christ-like. This is about learning the unforced rhythms of grace of being a disciple.

Hole 7

I Got Your Back

"Cast all your anxiety on him because he cares for you."
1 Peter 5:8

When I was coaching young girls in basketball, I could see the biggest problem for them was the fear of getting trapped with the ball and not being able to find anyone to help. Feeling alone and isolated, they would panic. Anxiety would grip them and the result would almost always be a double dribble, a walk, a bad pass, or the dreaded jump ball.

So, I taught our team to always keep one girl behind our player with the ball, providing an easy outlet pass in case of trouble and to always run to our player if she was in trouble. The peace this brought to our young girls was immediate. They rarely panicked. Instead, they could now see the court clearly and therefore make wise choices.

Their perspective was improved radically just by knowing there was always someone behind them, ready to take the pressure off of them. They thrived, they enjoyed the games, and they achieved their very best. The A+ life in sports!

This is what Jesus can and *wants* to do for you. I love the way Oswald Chambers puts it: "Fill your mind with the thought that God is there. And once your mind is truly filled with that thought, when you experience difficulties it will be as easy as breathing for you to remember, 'My heavenly Father knows all about this!'"

How would it change your life, your day to day decisions, if you knew you had someone always looking out for you? Times get tough and your anxiety is mounting. You are feeling trapped. The pressure is coming, and it's hard to "see the court clearly." How great would it be to know, with full and complete confidence, there is someone behind you waiting to take that ball of anxiety from you?

We humans have devised a multitude of safety valves that are poor substitutes for the real thing. They are not all necessarily evil, but they are always second rate. What do you rely on to give you this sense that you'll be taken care of?

Let me guess a few: your parents, your money, your job, your image, your stuff, your goodness, or your good works? Maybe it's keeping everything the same: your safe, but C- routine?

These may give us a sense of security, but they will always fail us when the press gets really tight. They will slip and slide beneath us. They are a sandy, not a solid foundation. That is why Jesus said, "Therefore everyone who hears these words of mine and puts them into practice is like a wise man who built his house on the rock. But everyone who hears these words of mine and does not put them into practice is like a foolish man who built his house on sand" (Matt. 7:24-27).

You are never alone when you have placed your trust in Jesus. He is always standing beside you saying, "Just relax. Hand those troubles over to me. I can take it. I got your back."

●

Hole 8

Grace Trumps Your Resume

"For whoever wants to save his life will lose it,
but whoever loses his life for me will find it."
Matthew 16:26

Have you ever flown first-class to Europe? It's a heavenly experience. These days, I focus on accumulating air miles for just that purpose. It's so natural to think of the good things we do as God-points we are accumulating, sort of like airline miles. We intend to cash them in on Judgment Day. If I received a notice that my miles no longer had any value, I would be incensed!

It's important to know that our good works do count for something. Of course they do. Just not for entry into Heaven. Think of them as spiritual style points, although this is not a fully satisfactory metaphor. And it's important to know that, as Dallas Willard said, "Grace is not opposed to effort; but to earning." So always give your best effort. Achieve your heart away. This is part of the A+ Life. But when surrender and grace trump all our efforts and achievements, that *is* the A+ Life.

Maybe this idea offends you, too. Maybe in church you nod your head along with everybody else when we say, "It's by faith in Jesus Christ and by faith alone." But inwardly, you're thinking, "Oh come on, God has to grade on the curve, at least some. He has to. It's not fair for my being good not to earn anything."

That's why Jesus says, "How hard it is for the rich to enter the kingdom of God!" (Luke 18:24). Allow me to rephrase what I believe Jesus is saying: "How hard it is for someone who has been so good, or has so much, to enter the Kingdom." The Kingdom is all about surrender. It's not about earning in order to get. It's about giving up in order to receive. Giving up, yes, but then receiving so much more, "immeasurably more than anything we could ask or imagine" (Eph. 3:20).

Save your resume, hold onto it for dear life, and your life will not be dear. Or, lose your resume and save your life.

53

Hole 9

Shame on You!

"There is therefore, now no condemnation to them which are in Christ Jesus,
who walk not after the flesh, but after the Spirit."
Romans 8:1

All of us heard this growing up: "You should be ashamed of yourself."
It wounds us so badly that we make it our goal to avoid that kind of
exposure at all costs. No one should have this attempt at guilt-
manipulation laid on them—not from another human. God is the only
one who can say this, and he won't. He didn't say it in the Garden, and he
doesn't say it now. It's not part of his original design. It's a human inven-
tion, designed to inflict painful suffering on the other.

When Jesus was confronted with the woman caught in adultery, he
didn't scold her and tell her, "I'm ashamed of you!"

He asked her, "Woman, where are they? Has no one condemned
you?... "Then neither do I condemn you," he declared. "Go now and
leave your life of sin" (John 8:10-11).

What are you hiding, and what are you using to hide behind? The
bottom line is that we are hiding our weaknesses, in whatever form. They
may be real, imagined, or just greatly exaggerated. But, I have news for
you: We all have weaknesses, so what's to hide? We are insecure human
beings just wanting people to like us.

After all the psycho-babble, it still boils down to this fundamental
human condition: we are afraid of being nakedly exposed for who we
really are, so we doggedly hide our true selves. Then, relationship havoc
ensues.

Our bushes and fig leaves are our many coping mechanisms,
masked by personality quirks and habits that cry out, "I won't let you see
the real me!" Loud or subdued... sarcastic or super sweet... crusty or
cream-puff... these act as garrisons: guarding our fear of exposure.

Some are obvious and some are deeply layered, but none are part of
God's design. They contribute to our conflicted relationships by making it

difficult to communicate without innuendos, tones, and looks—real or imagined. Even when there is no underlying desire to inflict shame, our past wounds scream, "Protect me!" So, we read into the other person's words a hidden meaning we are sure is meant to expose us and shame us.

The only way to be free of these insecurities—and ultimately these mindsets which hold us back from loving relationships—is to recognize that we are weak, frail, and imperfect. And that's ok! Jesus is strong where we are weak. When we allow him to come into every area of our lives, even the areas we are ashamed of, we allow him to transform us and provide us with the security and peace of his everlasting love.

Hole 10

Changed

"Can't you see the central issue in all this? It is not what you and I do—
submit to circumcision (change by works), reject circumcision.
It is what God is doing, and he is creating something totally new, a free life!"
Galatians 6:15, The Message

At the beginning of a new year, we typically think more about personal areas in which we'd like to improve. As the year moves on, as with life, we tend to sink back into our comfort zone and the idea of any radical change, well, it's just not that big of a deal anymore. "I'm okay, really. Oh sure, I could improve in that area, and I will! Just... later."

That, quite frankly, is a C- approach to life. Religion will do just that for you: a little change for the better... a little improvement in those nasty habits... at least, we get better at hiding those nasty habits. But, real change?

Forget change! Instead, embrace transformation. Change is a pedestrian approach. Change is for all the C-'s, and the world is full of them, as is religion. Let's seek transformation. We've already been formed spiritually, for better or for worse. That's why we need to be *trans*formed. The first step is not to make a plan.

Transformation comes through grace. Now, grace is not opposed to effort, but it is opposed to earning. So your "To Do" list is okay, just not the first step. The first step is to surrender: "Therefore, I urge you, brothers, in view of God's mercy, to offer your bodies as living sacrifices... Do not conform any longer to the pattern of this world, but be transformed by the renewing of your mind" (Rom. 12:1-2).

When we stop chasing what we are so sure will make us happy and surrender all that to God, we will look around one day and see that we have the true desires of our heart. And we didn't even realize that's what they were. We then see our desires were for a worldly C-, at best, but God gives us an A+: a transformed heart.

When we work after change, our life is improved, somewhat. But when we surrender to Jesus as our Savior and Lord, our life is enhanced. Your heart desires to be enhanced, not improved.

But remember, grace is not opposed to effort, just earning. So work up your "To Do" list. Just understand that it comes after the surrender. Improvement is the work of man; transformation is the work of God. Change solely by our own efforts produces a meandering creek. Transformation by Jesus produces overflowing streams of living water.

Hole 11

B.A.G.G.

"And He also told this parable to some people who trusted in themselves that they were righteous, and viewed others with contempt: Two men went up into the temple to pray, one a Pharisee and the other a tax collector... But the tax collector, standing some distance away, was even unwilling to lift up his eyes to heaven, but was beating his breast, saying, 'God, be merciful to me, the sinner!' I tell you, this man went to his house justified rather than the other; for everyone who exalts himself will be humbled, but he who humbles himself will be exalted."
Luke 18:9-14

The spiritual giant of this Biblical story is so obscure that we never learn his name. Though, he ranks with the best of the heroes of the faith. Jesus loved this guy. He is amazing. He impresses Jesus, not because of his good behavior, but because of his sorrow for his bad behavior. This self-proclaimed sinner recognized the condition of his heart. He was fully cognizant of his own, personal evil. No rationalizations. None of this, "I know I'm not perfect, but I'm not really *that* bad, either."

But, the other man in Jesus' story does, indeed, declare his goodness. He's not that bad; he's actually pretty good. Shoot, he's much better than most! Like a lot of us, he's a B.A.G.G.: "basically, a good guy." Jesus said, "The Pharisee stood up and prayed about himself: 'God, I thank you that I am not like other men—robbers, evildoers, adulterers—or even like this tax collector. I fast twice a week and give a tenth of all I get'" (Luke 18:11).

The key to finding God's grace through Jesus is to see, and see with painful clarity, your true sinful nature. "I'm not perfect" doesn't get it. Jesus didn't suffer the cross and pay the price for the "I'm not perfects" of this world. He marched up to that cross for those who are sick with sin... and know it.

I have known those who have come face to face with their sinfulness even while their cultural life was going well. Some have had to crash and burn to be able to finally see they are lost. It's not a one-size-fits-all formula, except for this one thing: "Lord have mercy on me, *the* sinner!"

Are you sick with sin? Are you sick of your sin? This is the first step into God's Kingdom. The narrow gate opens only to those who know they are sick and desperately want the cure. Clean and shiny, or dirty and grubby, the grace of Jesus is not for the pretty-goods, but for the "I need help's!"

Jesus said, "It is not the healthy who need a doctor, but the sick...For I have not come to call the righteous, but sinners" (Mark 2:17).

Hole 12

The Finest of Wines

"Taste and see that the LORD is good."
Psalm 34:8

Jesus and his pals are hanging out at a wedding reception. The wine is flowing, and the guests are having a big time throw down. (Who said the Bible is boring?) But suddenly, the wine runs out, and the hosts panic. Mary turns to Jesus and asks him to help. With just a nod, he changes the water to wine (John 2:1-11).

But this is bigger than just an amazing miracle. Buried in this story of Jesus' first miracle, which is recorded in the Gospel of John, are three words that give it 3-dimensional life.

First, the wine was the *finest*.

Second, the steward had to *taste* it to know this.

Third, John calls this miracle a *sign*. A sign points to something. A sign is meant to reveal information beyond just the shazam wonder of the miracle itself. So what does God, through John, want us to know about Jesus, through this sign?

What is he pointing to? The finest.

Everything Jesus does, everything he touches, is the absolute finest. No half effort from Jesus. No phoning it in for Jesus. Can you think of any situation in the stories of Jesus where he did anything half way? No, only the finest!

He fills Peter's nets with so many fish the nets almost burst. He feeds 5,000 families with so much food there are basketfuls left over. And all 5,000 families were nourished and full.

He heals completely all who came to him. Jesus never healed a lame person and said, "Well, that's the best I can do. Better get a cane to help with that lingering limp." Never! The lame man jumped up and down, dancing a jig. Lavish!

And so it will be with the *that* for which Jesus took hold of you, or, wants to take hold of you. Always the finest.

Let's dig deeper. After Jesus changes the water to the finest of wines, did anyone know it, yet? In an instant, this splendid wine is in the jars. But it required that the wine steward *taste* it to know how spectacular it truly was.

Jesus could have told the steward how incredible the wine was. He could have taught him how he changed the water to wine and described in detail its lavish essence. The steward, taking copious notes, would have known all about it.

But he had to taste it to truly know. And so do you. Too many of us know all about Jesus' promises. We know all about the lavish miracles. We even know all about him. But do you know *him*? Have you tasted his richness? Have you tasted his peace, his joy, his contentment? Maybe you have read all about these things, even memorized the passages. To take hold of *that*, for which Jesus took hold of you, you must taste his goodness. Not read about it. Not study it. Not attend classes or listen to sermons about it.

You must taste it.

Hole 13

Claim It

"...and everything that does not come from faith (trust) is sin."
Romans 14:23

After a few years in the grown-up world and accumulating a few disasters, we should come to the realization that the longer way around is usually the better way around. Even if we don't attribute this "It's always worth the wait" principle to God's way and God's plan for our lives, we still intuitively see that the quick fix is rarely, if ever, the best fix.

Why do we still take the shortcuts? Because we doubt God's goodness. We doubt his perfect love. We doubt he is watching or caring. Perhaps, we doubt he'll get involved in my particular situation. All temptations are simply shortcuts: a shortcut around God's plan for our lives. We want the instant gratification, so we convince ourselves through keen and splendid rationalization we both need it and we deserve it! We doubt God agrees or understands, so we take it.

And then, the temptation becomes the sin, which is not always about actions but is always about not trusting God's perfect love. If we are still thinking about sin in terms of actions and breaking rules, getting God mad, and getting punished, we are missing the whole point of grown-up sin.

Grown-up sin is not so much about actions as it is about our hearts. Our actions are only the symptom of the infection in our heart. Childish sins are about stupid actions; grown-up sins are rooted in distrust. Now, there are plenty of grown-ups pursuing the stupid childish sins to be sure. But whether they be neon-light sins or hidden-heart sins, grown-up sin is always about placing our trust in our favorite god: us.

Can we get a good working definition of sin, so we can get out of the sandbox of worrying about rules and getting in trouble with God to focus more on the infection in our hearts?

How about this definition: "... and everything that does not come from faith (trust) is sin" (Rom. 14:23). Everything that originates not from trust and confidence in God but from a heart infected with, "My claim to my right to myself," will result in sin every time.

Sin, not in the sense of breaking rules, but breaking the only bridge from our firmly entrenched position of "If I don't, it won't" and "What I must have to be happy," to the peace and contentment that can only be had through trusting God.

Until we surrender "our claim," we will not find the longer way around to God's grace and love. We will be living in sin, regardless of our squeaky clean or neon dirty actions. Surrendering my claim to trust myself is the only bridge across the chasm from our shaky self-confidence to confidence in God's perfect love.

Hole 14

Whoa, Easy Now

"For my yoke is easy and my burden is light."
Matthew 11:30

Let's play word association. What words come to mind when you hear, "Christian" or "Christianity?" Among the many, I bet that two didn't come to mind: rest and freedom. I'm also confident that two did, even if subconsciously: rules and performance.

Why did Jesus come? Have you given that much thought? If someone stopped you on the street, would you have a succinct answer? John, Jesus' best friend did. "The reason the Son of God appeared was to destroy the devil's work" (1 John 3:8).

Okay, so what was and is the devil's work? Always remember the 3 D's: Destroy, Distract, and Discourage. He does these masterfully through deceiving us. Satan wants us to think that the keys to the gates of heaven are in keeping the rules and performing well. He wants us to think the spiritual journey is about being *good enough* to qualify for heaven or not being bad enough to go to hell.

If Satan can keep us focused on rules and performance, then we'll miss the message of salvation, the Good News: it's not about *doing* because it's already *done.* Jesus did it. When we transfer our trust in our performance to Jesus' performance on the cross, we open the gates to salvation.

If you've found that relationship with Christ through His saving grace, Satan cannot destroy you. So, he'll spend the rest of your life seeking to distract and discourage you. How? "Keep the rules. Perform better. Build that Habitat House. Make pancakes for the church breakfast. Go to Sunday School, that's what counts. Do. Do. Do." How's that working for you?

When we inevitably fail at the rules or fall short of our *angry God's* performance expectations, we hear, "So, you really think you're a Christian? Who are you trying to fool? If people only knew. If you can't do any better than you'd best just give up, or at least stay away from God until He cools off." Recently, a friend who was beginning to see the Light, looked at me and said, "I'm worried that I won't be able to keep it all up, Sam." Confused, I asked, "Keep what up?" He said, "The Christian life I'm *supposed* to live."

Jesus understood this epidemic and sought to both encourage us and detox this poisonous religion. Yoke: easy? Burden: light? Are you kidding me? Being a Christian is hard *work*. What could He possibly mean?

When we read God's Word through this prism of rest, we will filter out the religious rules and see that, first and foremost, it's about a loving relationship. Jesus promises that this truth will set us free, free from the burden of performance. Free from the heavy rules mentality. Free to live our best life, motivated and energized by love, not guilt.

That's rest and freedom. Come on in, the water's fine!

Hole 15

For You – With You – Before You

"I press on to take hold of that for which Christ Jesus took hold of me."
Philippians 3:12

I want you to know God is *for* you, he is *with* you, and he is *before* you. In all things in all ways, he is for you. He looks at you and beams, "That's my child and I am well pleased with him, with her!" And he is always with you. He is even out before you, leading the way. When you "take hold of that," you will see him out before you, clearing the way, making your paths straight.

Following Jesus as we take hold of *that* means you are participating relationally and personally in his individual plan and purpose for you. It is not like wandering around in a big-box store, frustrated, and desperately hoping to sight an employee for some guidance and help. Because Jesus is for you, and he is with you, and he is out before you. Always.

Do you truly believe God is *for* you? Come on now, don't give me the Sunday School answer. You might assume he loves you because "God so loved the world" (John 3:16).

But do you think he *likes* you? Is he your friend? He does and he is. Taking hold of *that* means seeing that Jesus laughs with you, and smiles with you at your idiosyncrasies. He is pleased with you and proud of you even though you cannot possibly understand why. "That's my boy! Isn't he wonderful?" And, "Look at her. I'm so proud of her!"

Do you remember that poor girl caught in adultery and tossed down at his feet? Listen to Jesus' delicate response to her: "Jesus straightened up and asked her, "Woman, where are they? Has no one condemned you?"

"No one, sir," she said.

"Then neither do I condemn you," Jesus declared. "Go now and leave your life of sin" (John 8:10-11).

"I want you to 'leave your life of sin' because I am with you, and I will help you to do so. But 'neither do I condemn you,'" Jesus is saying, "Because I am way too much for you."

Jesus will not accept your sinful ways precisely because he is so for you. He knows how heavy and burdensome your sins and dysfunctions are, and he wants you to leave them behind. But this is a far cry from negative condemnation. Instead, he is calling you to follow him as he walks with you, and out before you,

May you allow Jesus to fully take hold of you as you press on to take hold of him, living "freely and lightly, learning the unforced rhythms of his grace."

Hole 16

Free or Slave?

"If you hold to my teaching, you are really my disciples.
Then you will know the truth, and the truth will set you free."
John 8:31-32

Do you typically associate the idea of *freedom* with being a Christian? Most would not. Most people associate these ideas with Christianity: "do this" and "you better not do that!" But, what was Jesus talking about when he said that the truth will set us free? I'm an American. I'm my own man. Free from what?

We can be set free *to* and be set free *from.* So, what would you really like to be free from? Or, to personalize this, what do you like least about yourself? Can't forgive, can't let go of the past, impatience, hard to feel good about yourself, hard to be quiet and alone, judgmental, envious, greedy, not content, those nasty habits… and no real peace?

Might these actually be holding you prisoner? No freedom in that. If we are after true transformation—which, of course, can only follow true surrender to Jesus—then we must look deeply into what we are holding onto. What we are holding onto might just be holding onto us even tighter, "for a man is a slave to whatever has mastered him" (2 Pet. 2:19).

What is the opposite of freedom? Slavery. And we are slaves to whatever has mastered us. "Well, I don't like that. I'm not a slave to anything." You may be. Your masters do not have to be neon light addictions; they may even be acceptable in our society. But, they could still be your masters. That which masters us can dictate, drive, and control us.

Slaves fear their masters. Why? Because their masters control their… happiness. And now, we have mined down to the core of this discussion of freedom and slavery: happiness. Is your greatest master, "What I must have to be happy?" Threaten that and watch the emotions rise: anxiety, anger, worry, stress, and conflict. They all howl with fear. Happiness, as with all feelings, is okay as a servant but disastrous as a master.

If you are a slave to happiness, you are a slave to fear (of losing that which makes you "happy"). Fear is rampant in our society. We are controlled by fear. We are driven by fear. We are mastered by fear. Indeed, we are driven to *react* in fear to our circumstances.

The truth Jesus spoke of earlier is that God loves you perfectly. Understanding this and appropriating it into our lives drives out all fear. When we embrace this wonderful truth, we are freed from fear and finally free to find *Life*. No longer slaves to fear, we learn to *respond* in faith (trust), knowing confidently that whatever is coming our way we can handle because it was allowed by a God who loves us perfectly.

"There is no fear in love. But perfect love drives out fear..." (1 John 4:18).

Hole 17

Quicksand

"As far as the east is from the west, so far has he removed our transgressions from us."
Psalm 103:12

Do you remember the old Tarzan TV shows? The safari crowd is moving through the jungle and suddenly someone steps in the dreaded quicksand. "Don't wiggle around!" Everyone knows doing that will just make you sink faster.

Is there really such a thing as quicksand? Yes, and you don't have to go to Africa to get stuck in it. It's called the Past and the Future.

And if you move around too much in either one you will surely sink faster.

I'm walking with my beloved Golden, Fannie, the other day, and I am one with the world. It's late afternoon, my favorite time to walk. The sun is fading, the shadows are falling, and it's quiet. The Upstate South Carolina air is incredibly fresh, and I am vibrating at a high frequency.

Suddenly, a memory of something stupid I did years ago sneaks into my present. The dreadful Past. "What an idiot," it whispers to me. "A Christian? Ha!" The Past accuses me scornfully.

I'm stuck in quicksand.

If I want to *"take hold* of that for which Christ Jesus took hold of me," I'm going to have to let go of the past. I'm going to have to let go of my own stupid and evil detours as well as what I perceive others have done to me.

But Satan will always seek to mire me in quicksand by reminding me and accusing me. Never forget his 3-D strategy: destroy, distract, and discourage. If he can keep you out of a saving relationship with Jesus, he will destroy your soul. Failing that, he will never stop trying to distract you and discourage you.

And he so often uses the Past and the Future. But you can let go of both of these because God is for you, God is with you, and God is before you. Your Heavenly Father wants you to appropriate his Divine Forgetfulness into your Present: "As far as the east is from the west." Satan doesn't want you to hear about that.

One thousand years later, God was still reminding us of his unfailing forgetfulness as Paul assuages our fears about our Past: "Once you were alienated from God and were enemies in your minds because of your evil behavior. But now he has reconciled you by Christ's physical body through death to present you holy in his sight, without blemish and free from accusation" (Col. 1:21-22).

When you surrendered and placed your full trust and dependence on Jesus, you were immediately washed clean of the Past. (You have surrendered, haven't you? If not, what in this world are you holding onto?) God then dropped your sins into a deep abyss and a "No fishing" sign popped up.

Your Father never goes back fishing into that abyss to revisit your sins. Only you can do that.

So stop it. Now! No fishing in the past anymore. Leave it there. God has.

Hole 18

Gifted

"…I have come that they may have life, and have it to the full."
John 10:10

We tend to think of spiritual gifts as the icing on the cake of the Christian life, when in fact, they are an intricate part of the cake. Spiritual Gifts are not reserved for just the "Special Christians." Through his grace, everyone who has surrendered themselves to Jesus is filled with the Holy Spirit. The Holy Spirit then brings vivid color to our monochrome lives, and our true personalities emerge through our spiritual gifts. The resulting life is, well, Life to the Full.

We get a list of some of the Spiritual Gifts in both Romans 12 and 1 Corinthians 12. You might want to read these passages, but here is a partial list: Prophecy, Service, Teaching, Encouragement, Leadership, and Mercy.

Scripture teaches us that we have a God-ordained purpose. He designed you and wired you for that purpose, and he wants you to live out your purpose on this earth. He is your #1 Fan, so he's rooting for you and is ready to help with the power of the Holy Spirit.

He is, as always, eager to say, "Well done, good and faithful servant!" (Matt. 25:21). Your Heavenly Father wants you to know you are his fine workmanship, crafted and "created in Christ Jesus to do good works, which God prepared in advance for us to do" (Eph. 2:10).

Now, to be sure, it is easier to serve God than to know him. Should I repeat that? Yes, it is so much easier to serve God—we love projects—than to take the time to know him.

So, I am cautioning you in advance not to grab your spiritual gifts and rush out to "work hard for God!" without first seeking his presence and his power. Busy projects result in a C- life, instead of the A+ Life to the Full. Jesus cautioned us to do this with him, looking to the Holy Spirit to do his job: to guide us and empower us from within.

He warned that doing it out of sheer will power, or worse, to serve out of a sense of "building my resume" will result in... nothing. Jesus said, "Remain in me, and I will remain in you... I am the vine; you are the branches. If a man remains in me and I in him, he will bear much fruit; apart from me you can do nothing" (John 15:4-5).

But, as we live out our natural, now supernatural spiritual gifts, we start to taste this Life to the Full. The energy of the Holy Spirit builds and thrives as we become integral and contributing parts of this energized, living, and breathing Body of Christ. Trust me, it's a whole lot more Life than you've been accustomed to.

C.S. Lewis calls your spiritual gift, "The secret signature of the soul."

Seek God's signature within you, live yours out, and you'll start living—for, perhaps, the first time—Life to the Full.

Round 3

Humility

"The better you putt, the bolder you play."
-Don January, Winner of 10 PGA Tour Titles

Hole 1

Me Christianity

"...Nevertheless, not my will, but yours be done."
Luke 22:42

Okay, for those of you who know me, this will come as no great revelation; but, it is always all about Sam. Me. The world revolves around me... in my mind. Just about every decision I make is filtered, consciously or subconsciously, through the "What's in it for me?" filter. Maybe the only time I put someone else's best interest in front of mine is with my daughter. The rest of you? You're on your own.

My guess is that most of us pursue a similar Narcissistic Christianity. Even if... *if*... we sincerely seek to follow, emulate, and worship Jesus, we are inwardly asking, "What's in it for me?" Have you ever left a church service and said something like, "Well, he was a little off today?" Or, "What was up with those hymns?" Or, "I didn't get anything out of that."

I confess that much of my talking and teaching is about what Jesus can do for one's life: the peace, joy, freedom, strength and power that He gives to us; the lavish life that He promises. I believe that. I know it to be true. I am living it.

But, that is akin to a 5 year old sitting in the stands at the World Series, thinking all the cheering is for him. We have an incredible disconnect between us, as the created, and God, the Creator. We're so important. Our *feelings* are paramount. God is our cosmic butler.

Oh, we would never say that. But, we live, pray, and worship that way. If we had a clue—just a clue—we'd fall prostrate before God, and worship in awe and wonderment at the cosmic majesty that He is. We'd gasp breathlessly anytime we thought of Jesus, talked about Him, or prayed to Him.

The Lord's Prayer is so familiar that it is undoubtedly the most *familiar* of all the rote recitations droned out by millions each Sunday. But, if we had a glimpse of His power and glory, we might not be able to get past the first words of the Prayer: "Our Father in heaven, hallowed be your name."

We'd stay on hallowed be your name, "all glory and honor to You, Father," until our minds grasp w*ho* it is we are approaching. Then, we might be better able to pray, from the heart, "Your kingdom come, your will be done, on earth as it is in heaven" (Matt 6:10).We might actually mean it. Certainly not *my* kingdom; please, not *my* will!

If we had a clue—just a clue—as to the power and majesty of God Almighty, El Shaddai, Creator of heaven and earth, our hearts would cry,

> Hallowed be your name,
> your kingdom come,
> your will be done,
> on earth as it is in heaven.

Hole 2

Deny Yourself

"Then he said to them all: 'Whoever wants to be my disciple must deny themselves and take up their cross daily and follow me.'"
Luke 9:23

Do you agree with the following statement? "Not all self is sin, but all sin involves self." To advance this thought, try substituting *self* when you see *sin* in scripture:

"Jesus replied, 'I tell you the truth, everyone who selfs ~~sins~~ is a slave to *self* ~~sin~~'" (John 8:34).

"But, if you do not do what is right, *self* ~~sin~~ is crouching at your door; it desires to have you, but you must master it" (Gen. 4:7).

"There is no difference, for all have *selfed* ~~sinned~~ and fall short of the glory of God" (Rom. 3:23).

I think it works, don't you? *Self* is constantly getting in the way of the "Life that is truly life." *Self* is a roadblock to "Life to the full."

Picture a social setting: people standing around chatting, meandering through the crowd, stopping to chat, and enjoying the festivities. But, if we could see the egos, the *selfs*—as they really are—they would be the 800-pound gorillas in the room. They would be clumsily pushing and knocking people aside, because, well, that's what *selfs* do.

When Jesus said, "If anyone would come after me, he must deny himself" (Luke 9:23), this is what he was talking about. In other words, Jesus was saying, "If you are going to follow me, to emulate me, to grow to be more Christ-like, you will have to deny your *selfs* when they attempt to crowd to the front of your life." To become more Christ-like is a series of self-denials, refusing to let *self* have its way.

Notice Jesus did not say, "He must deny himself 'things' or 'fun.'" Denying ourselves things may or may not come into play, but denying *self* is always the root issue.

If we cut the root of *self*, we will wither the tree of our sin. Imagine if you could actually defeat *self's* obnoxious whining: "What about me?

79

What's in it for me?" Worry? Fear? Greed? Pride? Anxiety? Anger? Lying, stealing, judging, and manipulating: these would all diminish as *self* diminishes, leaving the A+ life to be enjoyed. No *self*, no anxiety. No *self*, no pride. No *self*, no anger. No *self*, no judging. Imagine, just imagine.

With a heart lit up by Jesus' Light, we can start to see our *selfs* as silly little generals, proudly strutting around like the emperor with no clothes. Where is your *self* demanding its way in you? Where are you allowing *self* to crowd to the front and control your actions, and your reactions? Look for anxiety, anger, and… sin. That's where you'll find *self*.

Hole 3

The Resume

"'I tell you the truth, anyone who will not receive the kingdom of God like a little child will never enter it.' ...As Jesus started on his way, a man ran up to him and fell on his knees before him. 'Good teacher,' he asked, 'what must I do to inherit eternal life?'"
Mark 10:13, 17

The Rich Young Ruler approaches Jesus sincerely, but he is suffering from the most common and deadly of human ailments: a pretty darn good resume. He's a good person, but when he lays his head down at night, he is still haunted by doubt: "Is there more?"

We can see this right away with his first question: "What must I do to inherit eternal life?" He has his resume in hand and he's ready to have Jesus validate his qualifications so he can inherit life after death. The RYR wants to know, "How good is good enough?" He has his resume, and it's quite impressive. But here is his dilemma: Yes, he's been really good, but he knows in his heart this can't be all there is to it. There has to be more. So he seeks out Jesus to find this more.

"Jesus, I've kept all the commandments. Is there anything else I can be doing? I need some reassurance. Just give me a list and I'll do whatever it takes." Jesus could easily just remind him of what he had just said: "I tell you the truth, anyone who will not receive the kingdom of God like a little child will never enter it." Jesus is saying, "Doing is not the criteria. Receiving is." (Mark 10:17-27).

Like this successful young man, we would be confused and would press Jesus for more: "But that's not American, Jesus. We earn our way here. I can't even relate to this idea of just simply receiving. And this 'like a child stuff?'"

Jesus knows his heart and your heart, and his response is the same: "Jesus looked at him and loved him. 'One thing you lack,' he said. 'Go, sell... (surrender)... everything.'"

And now, lovingly, Jesus has him at a crossroads of faith, a spiritual crisis, and a chance for a defining moment in his life. Will he take it? Or, will he retreat back into his comfortable and well-earned, good-person life?

He just could not surrender his great resume and all the God-points he had accumulated. He is an achiever. Jesus is challenging him to redefine himself as a surrenderer, not as an achiever.

It's important to know that our good works do count for something. But we cannot do anything to earn salvation because it's already been paid for by Jesus. We simply surrender. We simply receive. But gosh, that's hard to do. It's just not that simple, is it?

In a defining moment, this young man refused to step into the Light. He actually said, "No," to God. He just could not surrender and receive… "like a child."

Not an easy thing to do. Not easy for a can-do man; not easy for a can-do American culture; not easy for a can-do church culture.

Can you surrender? Will you?

Hole 4

Garden Battle

"You will keep in perfect peace those whose minds are steadfast,
because they trust in you."
Isaiah 26:3

Approximately 2,000 years ago, Jesus walked into the Garden of Gethsemane, visibly shaken. Though, he walked out composed, confident, and courageous. What happened in that garden? Why the complete transformation?

Simply put, Jesus did battle with Satan, against Satan's favorite weapon, "self," and Jesus won. He emerged at peace.

Do you have peace today? Are you *at peace* day today? *Real* peace?

The Jesus we know and love—confident, composed, always in balance, and in harmony with himself and his Father—was none of these things as he entered the garden that Thursday night. He snapped at his best friends. He sweated bullets… blood bullets. He knew what was coming. He knew he was going to be beaten to a pulp. He knew he would endure unspeakable pain and agony. He knew that he would very shortly be absorbing your sins and mine.

In his humanity, he asked, "Is there another way, Father?"

And this is where Satan had come back to battle Jesus one last time. You may recall at the beginning of Jesus' ministry, after the temptations in the desert, "When the devil had finished all this tempting, he left him until an opportune time" (Luke 4:13). This was the opportune time.

I'm guessing Satan's opening gambit was, "Oh come on, Jesus, think about yourself for once. It's no sin. Be reasonable. Think about all the good you could continue to do if you go on living. There's got to be a better way than what God has planned. And think of the beating you're about to take. This could all be avoided if you'll just be sensible and logical and put yourself first for once."

But, Jesus would have none of it. Self knocked Adam and Eve out of the Garden. But it couldn't knock Jesus out of this garden. He battled

Satan and self, and he won. He did it for you and for me when he said, "Yet not my will, but yours be done" (Luke 22:42).

This is where he found "the peace that transcends all understanding" (Phil. 4:7). That's where you will find it, too: transferring your trust from yourself to your Father. There is only one way to this peace, and it is when we defeat self and come to the point where we can say with all sincerity, "Yet not my will, but yours be done." Can you say that? And truly mean it? It is not a one-time transaction, but it must begin with a *first*-time transaction.

Are you ready to do this? Are you ready for a garden battle? Be careful now. Do not do this lightly. If you really mean it, God will meet you in your garden. This is what Jesus did that night. It is why he went into the garden full of anxiety but emerged victoriously at peace. Are you ready?

Hole 5

Care – Free

"He said to them, 'Let the little children come to me, and do not hinder them, for the kingdom of God belongs to such as these. I tell you the truth, anyone who will not receive the kingdom of God like a little child will never enter it.'"
Mark 10:14

As I was walking Fannie, my Golden, around the neighborhood, I noticed four boys playing army. They were about six years old and completely engrossed in a battle against the *bad guys*, weapons in-hand. (When I was their age, against overwhelming odds, we fought off the Krauts to save America.) Here's what I *didn't* hear these kids saying as they were playing:

"I probably should go in and get to work. Fuel prices aren't getting any lower you know."

"Yeah, and I need to get ready for coloring tomorrow at kindergarten."

"Thanks for ruining it for me guys! You've reminded me of rising college tuition. Now I'll never get to sleep tonight!"

Like little children? What does Jesus mean by that? How could anyone operate in today's world like a child? I'm a man and a grown-up, so don't ask me to wimp out, start hugging trees and crying while opening up to my inner child. I don't think that is Jesus' message.

So what are the positive qualities of a child? Innocent, quick to forgive and forget, loving, living in the moment, uninhibited, playful... trusting and dependent... totally dependent.

The resounding quality I see is *carefree*. The kids at recess are playing care-free. They are not out there on the swings, worrying about math in fifth period. They are not playing kickball and stressing about bike payments. "Yes, Steve pulled my hair, and Jessie said I was a nerd, but that was *ten minutes* ago. I've moved on."

Why are they carefree? Because they *trust* their parents to take care of them. It would never enter their minds to not trust. It would never enter their minds to stress out and store up provisions for the future under the bed and in the closet. They *depend* on their parents, totally. They are carefree. They simply trust their parents.

We do not simply trust our Heavenly Father. We are not free of care. Of course we have to be responsible adults, and cares are going to come our way. It's what we do with those cares, and how long they stick to us that count. God urges us to *release* those cares to Him, casting them off like a fisherman throws a net out to sea.

The thief on the cross got it right: simple, not afraid to ask for help, totally dependent… recognizing Jesus as King. He said, "Remember me when you come into your kingdom."

Jesus answered him, "I tell you the truth, today you will be with me in paradise" (Luke 23:42-43).

Hole 6

Changed & Grateful

*"Humble yourselves, therefore, under God's mighty hand,
that he may lift you up in due time."*
1 Peter 5:6

If you were asked to give a description of a Christian— a disciple of Christ, not a person who just goes to a Christian church—what would you say? Notice I said a description, not a definition. I think I can capture the essence of a Christian in two words: changed and grateful.

I purposely did not describe a Christian as being "holy, righteous, loving, caring, peaceful, generous, or humble." A true disciple of Christ will become more and more like these, over time; but, the degree of is not the issue. The more telling description is that *something* happened, something changed. He or she may still be nervous, easily irritated, a tightwad, or whatever. Though, they will be *less* of that and will be changing to *more* of the above.

Prior to the first Easter, the disciples were focused on who's in the "greatest" group. John was even audacious enough to ask if he and James could have thrones next to Jesus. ("Let the rest of the brothers eat cake!") But he was changed.

"This is how we know what love is: Jesus Christ laid down his life for us. And we ought to lay down our lives for our brothers" (1 John 3:16).

Peter was so prideful that he bossed Jesus around. But he was changed. He said, "Humble yourselves, therefore, under God's mighty hand, that he may lift you up in due time" (1 Pet. 5:6).

James, Jesus' little bro, chided Jesus, mocked him, and dared him to go show himself in Jerusalem *if* he really was the Messiah. But James was changed. He began to refer to himself as, "James, a servant of God and of the Lord Jesus Christ" (Jam. 1:1).

Just to be clear, we're not talking about the kind of change that sometimes happens anyway as we get older: "I don't cuss as much, drink as much, fly off the handle as much, or lust as much." Nor are we talking about church starting to be more enjoyable: getting more involved because it's all warm and fuzzy to go to Bible studies, cook pancake breakfasts, and have all the kids at the Wednesday night suppers.

Jesus is talking about real heart change. A heart shift. You and I know the difference.

Hole 7

Rewards

"No one can serve two masters… You cannot serve both God and money."
Matthew 6:24

Okay, so I recently turned 35, and I'm feeling pretty good about life. I'm starting to make some real money, so I'm thinking about things I can buy… you know, as sort of a reward for my hard work.

But, I was at this gathering recently, and I couldn't help but overhear these two people talking. It turns out one was 85 and the other 50. They seemed engrossed in a discussion about "what's really important" and were lamenting that they had wasted a lot of time and spent a lot of money on things that had no eternal significance.

I overheard one of them saying, "I've been reading in the Scriptures, and it seems it really matters the way we handle our money here when we get there."

The other responded, "By *there*, you mean eternity? Because I recently read in Luke 16:9 where Jesus says, 'I tell you, use worldly wealth to gain friends for yourselves, so that when it is gone, you will be welcomed into eternal dwellings.' So, we should be purposeful and be smart with our money, investing it in Christian efforts?"

"Yes, that must be what he means!" said the older person. "And listen to what I saw yesterday in 1 Timothy 6:18-19. 'Command them to do good, to be rich in good deeds, and to be generous and willing to share. In this way they will lay up treasure for themselves as a firm foundation for the coming age, so that they may take hold of the life that is truly life.'"

Okay, so I'm listening to this stuff and trying to laugh it off, but I sort of feel like I'm nervously whistling in the dark. So I stirred up the courage to interrupt them: "Excuse me, I couldn't help but overhear you. I'm 35 and starting to make some real money. If you were me, how would you prioritize your spending and investing?"

The 85-year-old looked at me and said, "Do you remember what Jesus said about our money being our master? Because Jesus was saying we

89

will have a master, there is no avoiding that. The choice really boils down to either the Lord or Satan—and if it's Satan, count on him using your money as a trap."

He went on, "Whoever your Master is, he will have a hold on you. There is no better way to see who your Master is than to look at the way you spend your money. So, if you ask us, we'd say to set up your budget so you invest in the Lord's Kingdom first before you decide what to spend on yourself."

Are *you* giving God what's left over? Is that really what you want? If you think your cost of living is steep now, how do you think you'll feel about your cost of dying, then? Please make sure that you're not spending on a world that is going, instead of investing in a world that is coming. You might be missing an incredible and freeing joy. Break the grip!

Hole 8

A Yard Sale of the Heart

"Sell your possessions and give to the poor. Provide purses for yourselves
that will not wear out, a treasure in heaven that will never fail,
where no thief comes near and no moth destroys."
Luke 12:32-33

In what was a wondrously glorious time in my life, I moved eight times in eight years. Misery. And there were these five boxes I lugged from attic to attic. Eight times. I never even opened them. Just lugged them. "But, I might need whatever is in them… one day." With each move, they seemed to get heavier and heavier. I began to loathe them. I began to feel like a slave to those boxes.

So, finally, after the eighth move, I finally gave away what was inside the boxes. I had a yard sale. Gave it away. I was freed! What a cleansing experience.

Jesus told the Rich Young Ruler (RYR) to have a yard sale, too, if he wanted to be free to follow him. I have been told that Jesus' statement to the RYR about giving away everything was specifically for him. Nowhere else does Jesus say this to anyone. It is specific for the RYR because his money and his possessions ruled him. But, I was wrong.

Jesus says this elsewhere. As a matter of fact, he sort of makes it a universal principle—universal, as in, for all of us. Okay, don't panic. Or do. Whatever gets your attention. But, notice Jesus' words in this passage: "Do not be afraid, little flock, for your Father has been pleased to give you the kingdom. Sell your possessions and give to the poor" (Luke 12:32-33). Okay, now you can panic.

But, let's dig deeper. When Jesus tells the RYR (and us) to sell all and give to the poor, he is really saying, "Have a yard sale of the heart." He is saying, "Sell, give away, get rid of, run off, do whatever it takes to free yourself from whatever it is that has gripped you, that is holding you back from a full surrender to me. Then, you will be free to follow me."

Look at what Jesus says in this often overlooked passage about, yet again, having a yard sale of the heart: "Then the Lord said to him, 'Now then, you Pharisees clean the outside of the cup and dish, but inside you are full of greed and wickedness... But give what is inside the dish to the poor, and everything will be clean for you" (Luke 11:39, 41).

Shouldn't Jesus just say, "*Clean* the inside of the dish, like you do the outside?" Why does he add, "*Give* what is inside?" For that matter, why does he tell the RYR, as well as us, to give? Because Jesus knows our hearts, and he knows nothing competes for our hearts more than our money. Jesus knows the quickest way to start the process of surrendering to him is to start the process of *trusting* him. And nothing will force you to trust him more than to obey his commands to give, and give, and give.

Examine yourself today. Can you truly say that you have surrendered *everything* over to Jesus? Why not go ahead and have that yard sale. Trust me, you'll experience true freedom!

Hole 9

I'm Okay, You're Okay?

"Blessed are the poor in spirit, for theirs is the kingdom of heaven."
Matthew 5:3

After hearing the good-behaving, well-off Pharisee's carp for the umpteenth time about the company he kept, Jesus said, "It is not the healthy who need a doctor, but the sick" (Luke 5:31). The really good-behaving, "I'm doing fine" people have a hard time wanting to be helped by Jesus because they've done such a good job for themselves: "Who needs help? A little polishing-up maybe. But saving? Let's not get carried away."

Those who are sick want to get well... really want to get well. Those who are poor want help... really want it. They admit they are not okay. They know they need help. They know they cannot get there on their own.

But, those who are so sure they already have it? Well, not so much. Maybe that's why Jesus also said, "Blessed are the poor in spirit, for theirs is the kingdom of heaven" (Matt. 5:3). Jesus was saying, "I can only bless you when you recognize your spiritual poverty without me. Never mind your outward appearance, the show you put on for others. You know that, deep inside, you're bankrupt without me." So, do you need help? Do you want help?

Like the father with the demon-possessed son, let's declare, "I do believe; help me overcome my unbelief!" (Mark 9:24).

"I want to want. Help change my wants. I want to trust you. I want to know you. I want to love you. Help me overcome my not wanting, my not trusting, my not knowing, and my not loving! I want to know this guy, Jesus... really know him. I want to see with the eyes of Jesus. I want to feel with the heart of Jesus. I want to think with the mind of Jesus. I want to love with the love of Jesus."

Now, that would be the "A+ life.

Hole 10

The Hardest Thing

"Rest in the Lord, and wait patiently for Him."
Psalm 37:7

Waiting for God: it is perhaps the hardest thing to do for us busy, can-do, "If I don't, it won't" Americans. The complications we usher into our lives from ignoring this particular Holy Spirit guidance are so easily avoidable, but, oh so messy. Just think of the collapse that would have been avoided if Adam had said to Eve: "I know the fruit looks delicious, and maybe we did hear God wrong, or so the serpent says, but why don't we just wait and ask God?"

Jesus was emphatic about his disciples waiting for the Spirit's guidance and the Spirit's power. In the opening scene of Acts, we hear his admonition: "On one occasion, while he was eating with them, he gave them this command: "Do not leave Jerusalem, but wait for the gift my Father promised." But, I don't like to wait; I've got to act now! Waiting means I might not get my way. They need to hear my concerns, my superior advice: my complaints, corrections, and rebukes. I've got to keep everybody straight. If I don't *act*, this thing might get out of hand.

How many decisions have you felt compelled to act on, that, in retrospect, would have been so much better if you had just waited a while? How many comments have you made—of course, with the most sincere desire to help—that were so utterly ineffective, unnecessary, and destructive? Ignoring this rhythm of the spiritual life creates complications, hurt feelings, confusion, and suffering.

When I wait on God, I always see his best. When I wait on God and the guidance and power of his Spirit within me, the result is always the best. Not sometimes… always. When I refuse to wait, I grieve his Spirit within me. Waiting on the Spirit's guidance brings me closer to my Lord… every time. I get to see his movement. I get to see his power at work. None of which are possible when I am acting on my own impulse.

God tells us, "Be still and know that I am God" (Psalm 46:10). Oh, to be still. To know God.

Jesus reinforces this ridiculously impractical counsel with, "The pagans run after all these things, and your heavenly Father knows that you need them. But... (wait)... and seek first his kingdom and his righteousness, and all these things will be given to you as well" (Matt. 6:32-33). It's safe to wait, if you live in a God-saturated world. It's safe to wait, if you see the Holy Spirit permeating your life.

"The pagans run after these things." Notice that Jesus didn't say, "The horrible sinners run after these things." Pagans are those who don't know God. They are scurrying and running, not waiting. They are acting and reacting... busily. I've been a pagan long enough. I want to know God. So, I'll learn to be still, and to wait.

Hole 11

The Journey

*"Whoever sows sparingly will also reap sparingly, and whoever sows generously
will also reap generously... for God loves a cheerful giver."*
2 Corinthians 9:6

Never mind about the freedom and the joy, the satisfaction and the reward of giving: if God loves a cheerful, generous giver, I want to be one! But, let's dig deeper. There is an eternal perspective to giving that most overlook. If you get this, if you embrace this eternal perspective, your life will change. You will thrive with a financial freedom few ever attain.

Jesus pulls back the curtain on eternity and gives us a vivid glimpse into the direct correlation between how you spend your money *here* and how you will spend eternity *there*. Notice that I did not say *where* you will spend eternity, but *how*.

Let's start with Jesus' conclusion to his parable about the rich fool, who was a stingy man: "Sell your possessions and give to the poor. Provide purses for yourselves that will not wear out, a treasure in heaven that will not be exhausted..." (Luke 12:33). Jesus is saying that every time you give generously here, you are actually investing in a heavenly IRA, with an eternal interest rate return that blows the doors off anything here. This sounds a tad self-serving, doesn't it? Is Jesus actually saying our giving *here*, is tied directly to rewards *there*?

There's more: "I tell you, use worldly wealth to gain friends for yourselves, so that when it is gone, you will be welcomed into eternal dwellings" (Luke 6:19). What is this "worldly wealth" to which Jesus refers? Your money. And who is going to welcome you into heaven? Those who benefited from your generous giving.

Now, just imagine stepping into heaven, and people from all walks of life come up to you and thank you for giving to a cause that benefited them. If you get this, if your heart is invaded and absorbed into the generosity Jesus is promoting here, you will never be the same. You will never again be mastered by your money and, even more, you'll actually be looking around for ways to invest in God's Kingdom. Not only will you *not* cringe when that request for help comes, you'll be proactively looking for it.

My dear friend, Dan Weathers, exemplified this generous heart. Dan didn't make much money, so when he told me he planned to invest $20 a month in 721 Ministries, I said, "Thanks Dan. But you don't need to do that. I know money's tight." Dan wheeled around and exclaimed, "Oh no, don't you dare rob me of this blessing!"

Dan understood the principle of giving on earth to invest in the eternal kingdom. Can you imagine the welcome Dan received when he stepped into his eternal dwellings, built on the firm foundation of his generosity while on earth?

I want that. Don't you? So, be generous. Be smart about it, and invest wisely, but invest generously.

Hole 12

Green Lights – Red Lights

"But when he, the Spirit of truth, comes, he will guide you into all the truth."
John 16:13

Jesus promises a life of clarity, energy, and creativity through the Holy Spirit. I want this, don't you? I need this guidance. Please do not tell me you don't. Acts is replete with example upon example of the Holy Spirit doing precisely what Jesus said He would do.

He guides the apostles with green lights: "While they were worshipping the Lord and fasting, the Holy Spirit said, 'Set apart for me Barnabas and Saul for the work to which I have called them'" (Acts 13:2). The Holy Spirit encourages Peter with a green light: "Yes, definitely go see Cornelius, the outsider Gentile. It's okay, it's part of my plan" (Acts 10:19, paraphrased).

The Holy Spirit convicts and protects the Apostles with red lights: "Paul, do not go to Asia. I have other plans for you" (Acts 16:6-10, paraphrased). Paul hears the Holy Spirit's green and yellow light: "And now, compelled by the Spirit, I am going to Jerusalem, not knowing what will happen to me there. I only know that in every city the Holy Spirit warns me that prison and hardships are facing me" (Acts 20:22-23).

Did you know that you can live your life knowing God's will for you day to day? Are you aware God promises this clarity and insight, step by step? You can walk through life sensing God's movement and will as you encounter conversations, conflicts, challenges, and decisions. With the Holy Spirit guiding you into all truth, this powerful gift is already within you. Notice that Jesus promised the Holy Spirit would *guide* you. The Way of Jesus through this powerful Holy Spirit is to guide you, not frog-march you into a set of dogmatic doctrines and rules. This is the gentle rhythm of the Holy Spirit, guiding but not forcing.

The last night Jesus is with his boys, he tells them, "You've been with me three years. You have followed me. Now, just keep following my Way." Thomas replied, "We don't know the way" (John 14:5-7, paraphrased). Thomas was saying, "We know the rules, but we don't know the way!" Jesus then makes his heart-piercing declaration: "I am the Way, I am the Truth, and I am the Light" (John 14:6). Wouldn't you rather follow Jesus than follow rules? Wouldn't you rather be guided and directed by Jesus' Holy Spirit than to try real hard to follow a list of directions? Yes, there are "rules," and there are commandments. But they are given to protect us, not prohibit us.

Jesus can see that you will sometimes become frustrated and exasperated. He is saying to you, today, "Just follow me. I'll show you the Way. And I will give you the Power within to guide you. The promise is about walking in rhythm with your Lord. But you must surrender your insistence on your own way. You must surrender your will to the way of Jesus.

Hole 13

The Big Head

"For although they knew God, they neither glorified him as God nor gave thanks to him, but their thinking became futile and their foolish hearts were darkened... They exchanged the truth of God for a lie, and worshiped and served created things rather than the Creator..."
Romans 1:21, 25

My daughter doesn't appreciate just how great I am. And she sure doesn't appreciate what a tremendous athlete I... maybe... used... to be. Any time she senses my ego rearing its ugly head, she puffs up her cheeks, puts her hands to the side of her head, and starts to expand them outward: "Dad's head is getting bigger, again." Busted!

I see in this a telling worship analogy. Picture God as this huge, bright, and shining sun. And next to this huge, massive God, place yourself as a tiny—and I mean tiny—stick figure; no more than a dot, really. Now, this is the appropriate comparative imagery, if God is God, that is. If God is God, we are just not such hot shots, are we? I think our worship might take on a different perspective if we kept this imagery in proper focus.

Yet, we humans are so important! The universe revolves around us. We shrink God down to 25 watts and blow ourselves up to King Kong size. We reverse the proper image: massive us, puny God. Guess where the emphasis on worship shifts? I become my own idol. Being *happy*, getting what I want... idols.

When John the Baptizer was approached by his disciples— expressing their concern that this new guy, Jesus, was baptizing more than John—he put it succinctly: "The bride belongs to the bridegroom. The friend who attends the bridegroom waits and listens for him, and is full of joy when he hears the bridegroom's voice. That joy is mine, and it is now complete. He must become greater; I must become less" (John 3:29-30).

Here's the life application. If we are moving through life with the appropriate perspective—God as huge and us as tiny—we would be naturally inclined to worship Him just for who He is: God Almighty! He is worth it, and worthy of it. Unless we are mindless Neanderthals, our hearts naturally pour out to Him, from the inside-out, with awe, wonder, and adoration.

We begin to sense the awe of His power. We wonder at His perfection. Our hearts then pour out adoration for a Heavenly Father who loves us as we are: sinners.

The truly rich Life in the Kingdom is to worship God, shrink our egos, love people, and use things. However, most of us shrink our perception of God, worship ourselves, love things, and use people.

I want to learn to worship God from the inside-out: heart first, and then my head follows. I'm tired of worshipping the big head. I'm weary of worshipping my little wants. Are you?

Hole 14

Authorized

"Then Jesus came to them and said,
'All authority in heaven and on earth has been given to me.'"
Matthew 28:18

Recently, I was pulled over and ticketed—unfairly!—by a highway patrolman. In that moment, I greatly resented his authority over me. Then, a friend told me about his daughter being saved, literally rescued, from a dangerous situation by the bravery of a highway patrolman. (Probably not the same one who stopped me...)
I was so moved, and thanked God for that patrolman's position of authority that he exercised so heroically.

The difference? At first, I was controlled by pride and ego: "Who is this guy to be in a position over me? I don't need this." My friend was motivated by an awareness of his daughter's need—acute need—for this man in authority to save her. I *bristled* at his authority over me while she was more than happy to *surrender* to his authority.

Authority is the power or the right to control, command, or determine. It can also be an accepted source of information, advice, etc. Who are the authority figures in your life? The obvious: your boss, clients, parents, spouse, the government, the IRS, and officers of the law. But, have you really thought about those hidden authorities... the presence of power that exercises control over you?

How about the culture? "You deserve to be happy, so just charge it all to your MasterCard!" Maybe success is your authority, the terms of which are dictated by culture and society.

For many of us, the principle authority in our lives is, "My claim to my right to myself." It's an *addiction*, actually. For most of my life, I know I've been addicted to the idea that things should, and must, go the way I want them to go. That addiction has been a huge authority in my life. It has exercised control over my thoughts, my decisions, and my emotions... typically, not to my benefit.

What is your authority? Please think deeply about this. It matters! Who speaks with authority in your mind? Is it what or who you would really want it to be? Or have you given this authority to someone or something that—well, if you wrote it down in black and white—you'd be mortified that you somehow had allowed this to happen?

Peter said it best: "'Lord, to whom shall we go? You have the words of eternal life. We believe and know—have come to know—that you are the Holy One of God" (John 6:68). We've all gone to many other places—some intentional, some without realizing it—looking for an accepted source of information, advice, etc. The more I continue on this spiritual journey, the more I see the obvious: God, alone, has the words of eternal life. Only Him.

So, who is your final authority? In the inner recesses of your mind, when no one else can know what thoughts you are processing, who is in control?

Hole 15

My Way or the Highway

"Be still, and know that I am God."
Psalm 46:10

We all start life with a "My Way" type of affliction. For some, it becomes a neon light obsession; for others, it's more subtle. But, it is there for all of us, and it is self-defeating, even as it seeks to keep self in control. The longer we live with this *My Way affliction*, the more damage we cause. Sooner or later, we all have to come face to face with God, and either surrender our claim to our way, or...not.

Doing it our way, insisting on our way, is a recipe for disaster. The road to self-determination is littered with the ruins of personal, as well as collateral, damage. The highway to "I did it my way" is strewn with the wreckage of self, self, self—and those whose lives were damaged by the My Way types.

Jesus warned us about this affliction and the consequences: "For whoever exalts himself will be humbled, and whoever humbles himself will be exalted" (Matt. 23:12). And he encouraged us to rise above it: "Also a dispute arose among them as to which of them was considered to be greatest. Jesus said to them, 'The kings of the Gentiles lord it over them... But you are not to be like that. Instead, the greatest among you should be like the youngest, and the one who rules like the one who serves'" (Luke 22:24-26).

For the earlier part of my life, I insisted on being the boss. This included 10 years after Jesus saved me. What an idiot. As a young girl, my daughter would defiantly say to her schoolyard friends, "You're not the boss of me!" As a grown-up, I've said the same thing to God, just more subtly: "It's got to be my way, God, for me to be happy." He eventually responded, "Okay, have it your way, Sam." Ugh.

And I'm not alone. The Bible is filled with these, "My way, not yours" types, with Jacob being the poster boy. He tricked his aging father, Isaac, as well as his brother, Esau. He did it his way. Yes, he got his way.

But he and those around him paid a costly price: a 50 car pile-up that took twenty years to unravel. And a disjointed hip. Jacob was finally ready to give up his way but only after getting alone with God, one-on-one, just Jacob and God. And so it must be for each of us.

We "Christians," are fond of saying, "Jesus is my Lord and Savior." But sometimes, we don't have a clue. If he's our Lord, then he's our boss. He's a loving, caring, compassionate, and fun boss; but, he's still the boss—and don't miss this: we want him to be. If he's our Lord, we gladly surrender all voting privileges to him. If he's our Lord, we don't even consider ourselves to be on the management committee.

Don't insist on being the boss. Surrender that role to Jesus. We stand the tallest when we are on our knees in surrender. And one way or another, in this life or the next, you will kneel in surrender.

Are you still the boss of you?

Hole 16

Not Weak, but Meek

*"Do nothing out of selfish ambition or vain conceit. Rather,
in humility value others above yourselves, not looking to your own interests
but each of you to the interests of the others."*
Philippians 2:3-4

Who is the #1 troublemaker in your life? Who causes the most stress? Think of a name. Which person in your life, if they would just quit doing whatever it is they are doing... if they would just quit being who they are being... if they would just have a heart change... your life would be so much better? Think about this for a moment. Got someone in mind? I bet you do.

I don't even have to know you to know the correct answer: you.

You are the common denominator in all your problems, in all your conflicts, and in all your stresses. You are the #1 troublemaker in your life. Oh sure, no doubt *they* share in the blame. But, come on, you and I know that it's you, and it's me. More specifically, it's our heart.

Jesus couples his, "Blessed are the poor in spirit" (Matt. 5:5), with an even more unsatisfying pronouncement: "Blessed are the meek" (Matt. 5:3). These two are related by cause and effect. Once we have been convicted of our spiritual poverty apart from Jesus and have cried out to be rescued by him, it is hard to be puffed up about oneself. These two both emanate from the same kind of heart: a heart touched and softened by God's stunning grace through Jesus.

Meekness is not an attitude; it's a heart condition. Being meek does not mean you think poorly of yourself. It means you are less and less interested in thinking about yourself at all... and more and more about others. A meek heart is guided not by the mirror but by the Messiah.

A meek person is not a weak person. To the contrary, he or she is empowered by Jesus with a quiet strength, and a humble, but strong confidence. As in all of Jesus' teachings, a meek heart opens the key to the A+ life Jesus wants for you.

Meekness doesn't says, "Look at me, aren't I good!" Meekness says, "Look at them, aren't they great!"

When things go awry, meekness doesn't say, "Where are they wrong?" Meekness says, "Where am I responsible?"

When in conflict, meekness doesn't say, "I know I'm right." Meekness says, "I might not be completely right about this."

A meek heart easily and naturally says, "You're more important than me," not because of a low self-image, but because of a new crystal clear self-image, viewed through the lens of Jesus as Rescuer, Master, and King. A heart softened by saving no longer *wants* to think first about itself. It has been freed by Jesus to live unencumbered by the burden of being so important. Have you?

May you find this freedom to think more about others and less about yourself through the transforming meekness of Jesus Christ.

Hole 17

A Story of Meek Strength

"So in everything, do to others what you would have them do to you,
for this sums up the Law and the Prophets."
Matthew 7:12

When Jesus said, "Blessed are the meek," there must have been a lot of confusion about what he meant by *meek.* I can imagine many of the men stiff-arming the idea of acting timid and weak, and the women trying so hard to play the role of the meek wife, but throwing the frying pan at their knucklehead husbands instead.

I know of a man who epitomizes what it means to be meek. He's a rough-around-the-edges kind of guy, making his living in a small town as a craftsman. He's certainly not weak. He was engaged, but his bride to be turned up pregnant before their marriage. He was devastated: hurt, angry, betrayed, and humiliated.

He had his life so planned out. Everything was going along according to his plan. He had worked hard to save the money for her dowry, proudly presenting it to her father at the time of the engagement. Now, it was all ruined. How could this have happened to him? What would the village think?

In their culture, he could be stoned to death if they think he got her pregnant. His friend gave him this advice: "It's best to divorce her and be sure to make a public spectacle of it. She ruined your life, man, and she should pay for it." Well, that made perfect sense to the man. But, gosh, she would suffer mightily if he did it that way. Her life would be ruined. She might even be killed.

That just didn't feel right in his heart, even as broken as it was. His choice was to either divorce her quietly, which meant he would forfeit his right to getting his dowry back—his life savings—or do it publically. Doing it publically would get his money returned, as well as his reputation. If he did this quietly, his reputation would surely suffer even though he was confident everyone knew he was a decent man—some even called him righteous. He was nothing special, just a man who wanted to please God as well as look out for others when he saw the chance.

Earlier in his life, he had been more self-absorbed, always thinking of himself first. Then, God had helped soften his heart, and it felt so good to put others first. Whenever his patience was running thin, or his personal agenda impeded, he just reminded himself, "They're just as important as I am." What a difference in his life!

As he contemplated his options, he couldn't help but think about his poor fiancé. Who was he to ruin her life? Yes, he was angry, and hurt and embarrassed, but he had done some really stupid things in his life, too. How would he feel if all his stuff was put on display?

Right then and there, he knew what he had to do. He considered the good of his fiancé above himself. He thought to himself, "Who knows, maybe this child will learn from this and put others first as well."

What would you have done?

Hole 18

Bankrupt!

"These are the ones I look on with favor:
those who are humble and contrite in spirit..."
Isaiah 66:2

Jesus makes an opening salvo in his Beatitudes that has caused many a man to stiff-arm the whole idea of following Jesus... or, maybe I should say, *seriously* following him. When he says, "Blessed are the poor in spirit, for theirs is the kingdom of heaven" (Matt. 5:3), men—especially men—tend to push back on the mistaken idea of having to act poor or be poor!

There is nothing in our culture that supports anything other than being *the man*: rich in all ways, especially in self-confidence, and with an "I'll conquer that mountain" attitude. We bring this same mindset to our spiritual lives. As much as we might verbally agree that we can't earn our way into heaven, the unspoken conspiracy is, "But, I can. Surely I must be able to, at least a little."

We see this even in the language we use about salvation: "I *accepted* Jesus. I *made a commitment* to Jesus." As if we studied the issue, weighing all our options, and then graced Jesus with our assent. We agreed to allow him into our lives? We condescended to join his club? Ha!

Jesus is saying this simply won't work in his Kingdom. Jesus is saying this attitude locks us out of the Kingdom. He is also saying we hold the key. And this key, for men as well as women, is in his first Beatitude.

When Jesus says, "Blessed are the poor in spirit," what he's actually saying is "When, and only when, you recognize your spiritual poverty apart from me, will your heart cry out for help." Until we come to this startling reality that we are spiritually bankrupt, who needs a Savior?

"Oh sure, I'm not perfect," we say, "but, I'm actually not that bad," we whisper. "And anyway, a fair God grades on the curve, right?"

But, no, I am spiritually bankrupt, and I bring nothing... nothing at all. This is not a decision we make after much intellectual navel-gazing; it is a stark reality that cuts to our core. It is much like the reaction of the people in Jerusalem after hearing Peter's Pentecost sermon: "When the people heard this, they were cut to the heart and said to Peter and the other apostles, 'Brothers, what shall we do?'" (Acts 2:37)

At different points in our lives, we come face to face with our sinful condition. At some point, we cry out, "What shall we do?" We become cut to the heart, or we harden our hearts just a little more and say, "I'm doing alright." But, come on, you really are not.

May you experience the gift of realizing your utter spiritual bankruptcy. Then, may you experience the incredible freedom of surrendering to the only true King.

Round 4

Integrity

*"A good player who is a great putter is a match for any golfer.
A great hitter who cannot putt is a match for no one."*
-Ben Sayers, Golf Instructor for British Royalty

Hole 1

Shortcuts

"Delight yourself in the LORD and
he will give you the desires of your heart."
Psalm 37:4

How do we slide from joy and contentment to temptation and sinning? What begins that process? If we can identify the warning signs, we might be better able to blow up the bridge before we—or the enemy—gets across it.

The slide begins with doubt: a waning of trust. And what exactly is it that we are doubting? God's control. God's sovereignty. God's perfect love. So, in our doubt, temptation rears its ugly head, and we slide towards fear. As we find ourselves in the fear zone, we start to press and hurry. We are pressing and hurrying for one thing: to make sure *our will is done*.

All temptations represent shortcuts. Shortcuts to what *we* want… to getting our way… to getting our will to be done… not God's. Why? Because we don't trust God's will, God's plan, or God's goodness. To be blunt, we *fear* God's will.

Eve saw the fruit, and it was *pleasing to the eye* (Gen. 3:6). I bet it was. I can imagine her thought process: "I need it. I deserve it. I've got to have it… *now*." There is a lot of *now* in the slide from joy to temptation to sin. There is much hurrying, too. That's why we call temptation, *shortcuts*. We see, we like, and we want. So, we step outside God's plan, we circumvent His timing, and we go get it.

What tempts you? Where is your bridge defense the weakest? Many of you aren't tempted by the big neon light sins: robbing a bank, murder, or adultery. But, in our hearts, we are tempted to secure more money, to dislike with contempt, and to leer with the purpose of lusting. Or maybe yours is judging, holding a grudge, not forgiving, controlling, self-vindication, counter attack, lying, or gossiping.

115

Adam and Eve made two mistakes in the Garden. The first was to engage in a conversation with Satan. Huge mistake. That's one that we often make. Of course, we don't see it that way. But, the one-sided conversation goes like this: "You like that." Then, "You need that." Keep sliding: "You *deserve* that." "You need to get that… now!"

The second mistake was for Eve to lock her gaze on the object of her desire. Move your gaze. Close the door on that which is the object of your desire. Arnold Glasow said, "Temptation usually enters through a door that has been intentionally left open."

There is a certain amount of self-discipline involved in defeating temptation, but the long-term solution is a changed heart. We need a heart that is so full of God's grace and love that we see the temptation, and we're just too content to be interested.

The real solution: "Delight yourself in the LORD and he will give you the desires of your heart" (Psa. 37:4).

Hole 2

What Were You Thinking?

*"Those who live according to the sinful nature have their minds set
on what that nature desires; but those who live in accordance with the Spirit
have their minds set on what the Spirit desires."*
Romans 8:5

We are all in the process of evolving: emotionally, mentally, and spiritually. I suggest that this process is taking place in the mind and the heart. But, is one feeding the other? Are they evolving in sync, or is one a source for the other?

God cautions us, "Above all else, guard your heart, for it is the wellspring of life" (Prov. 4:23). A wellspring is a source. When used in our writing and speaking, it typically implies an inexhaustible source. And Jesus says, "For out of the overflow of the heart the mouth speaks" (Matt. 12:34).

I snap at my daughter or swear at that driver in front of me, and I wonder, "Where did *that* come from?" It came from my very own dark heart. And I believe that the source for our hearts is our minds. My mind is what feeds my heart.

For a several years, I have been asking God to change my heart. I simply cannot *will* that to happen. But, I can control my thoughts. What we think about, and how we think about it, colors the flow into our hearts.

When I was developing communities back in the 80's, I learned that golf course ponds were typically colored with a greenish blue dye. I started doing that for my lakes and ponds, and the results were terrific. But, I had to periodically add the dye to maintain the pretty color. What if I could have changed the source flowing into my lakes?

Isn't that what we do? We like to dye our lives so that we look pretty: nice, caring, smart, together, and even holy. Yet, we fail to change the source; it becomes a repetitious, tiring treadmill. If I change the source

117

flowing into my heart, my thoughts, then I'm giving God an assist in His process of transforming my heart.

So, what do you think about? Rene' Descartes famously surmised, "I think, therefore I am." May I take it one step further and say, "What one thinks, plays a major role in what one does?" We think about what is important to us, and it is a universal truth that what's important to us gets done. Further, what I do with my life becomes my legacy.

So, I'll ask again: What are you thinking about? Are your thoughts and mind a wellspring of life... or a polluted source of darkness?

Hole 3

Satan's Opening Strategy Session

"Do not be conformed to this world, but be transformed by the renewal of your mind,
that by testing you may discern what is the will of God,
what is good and acceptable and perfect."
Romans 12:2

Imagine Satan and his cohorts in their opening strategy session:
Satan: "Okay, guys, give me some ideas on our attack plan against God."
Demons: "Attack God? Are you insane? We tried that. *You* tried that, and look what happened!"

"Of course we're not going to attack God directly, at least not for now," says Satan. "But, we know his Achilles heel is his prize creation... those humans he loves so much. So, if we can hurt them, we can hurt him—badly. So, let's strategize."

"Well," a demon answers, "the humans consist of body, mind, and spirit. So, any effective attack should be against one or more of those areas. If we can get at them through one, we tend to get the other two. They mistakenly think the three are separate; that the body, the mind, and the spirit are independent of each other. Can you imagine that?"

"Brilliant! You're dead on it. Let's go after each of those three, but let's do it with subterfuge," Satan replies.

"Subterfuge? What do you mean? Espionage?"

"Not quite. One of the great weapons in any warfare is to distract the enemy. With the social cultures that we're going to dominate, it will be easy to just ease them away from God, bit by bit. We'll blind them to the cumulative effect of all their little decisions. Before they know it, they'll have drifted so far away, the effort to get back will be too much. They'll have become so comfortable with their status quo that most of them won't even see how far they've drifted from what they would say are the truly important things."

Satan continues, "Even if they do realize just how far they've drifted away from the things that used to be important to them, they won't have the will or the energy to affect any change, and we'll have them. It will be so easy. You see, we convince them that this little decision today—or, better yet—this little *no decision* today, really is insignificant in the grand scheme of things: 'It's no big deal. I'll get back to a little more discipline... later.'"

"Soon, they will be too busy for any meaningful quiet time with their Creator. I know it seems utterly ridiculous that we could convince them they have no time to set aside each day for the one who created them and loves them, but just watch how easy it will be."

Sounds pretty familiar, huh? How many of us have fallen prey to these tactics? I hope this gets you thinking about the importance of time and how you spend yours. It's the little things that count!

Hole 4

The Narrow Road

"Enter through the narrow gate. For wide is the gate and broad is the road that leads to destruction, and many enter through it. But small is the gate and narrow the road that leads to life, and only a few find it."
Matthew 7:13-14

All temptations are simply shortcuts: a shortcut around God's plan for our lives in order to grasp the glittery apple of short-term happiness. We want the instant gratification. We see it, and we want it. We rationalize that we really do need it. And finally, the coup de grace, we convince ourselves, "I deserve it!"

How's that been working out for you?

We think, "If I don't, it won't." She's not doing right. He hasn't changed a bit. The check is not in the mail, and things are not getting any better… as per my timing. So if I don't fix her, change him, force the issue, control the outcome, or control it, him, her, or them… it won't happen like I am sure it must!

So, I'm tempted to snap, to criticize, to freeze out, or to self-defend. I overreact. I worry. I stress-out myself and everyone around me, all because I thought, "If I don't, it won't."

We are driven to take shortcuts by our obsession with our own happiness. I deserve to be happy, and I sure don't deserve the ways things are going. So I'll reach out and bite the apple of instant gratification. I'll worry about the consequences later. Above all else, my feelings must be satisfied because I must feel happy, whatever it takes.

If they only knew what I put up with… what I am going through… how unique my situation is… they would understand. Besides, it's my life, and I'm king. I know what's best for me. Me… Me… Me…

In conflict, in worry, or in a hurry, as well as in lust… it's really all about trust. Do you trust God? Do you trust that he loves you perfectly? Do you trust that his timing will ultimately be just right?

Do you trust that he is in charge of her, him, or it? Do you trust that if you wait patiently for God to move, the end result will always be infinitely better?

Do you trust that God's way brings a pervasive joy, not just temporary happiness?

Or, is this kind of trust just not practical in your world, so you must trust… yourself?

Hole 5

Feeling or Thinking?

"Do not love the world or the things in the world. If anyone loves the world, the love of the Father is not in him. For all that is in the world—the lust of the flesh, the lust of the eyes, and the pride of life—is not of the Father but is of the world."
1 John 2:15-16, NKJV

All of our shortcuts are simply a transfer of trust: from God to ourselves... from God's plan to our plan... from God's timing to ours. We think we know the desires of our hearts. We are sure of what they are, and we must have them to be happy.

God comes along and says, "You don't even know what your true desires are. This culture has blinded you. But if you'll let me... if you'll trust me... I can guide you to them."

You will be the most surprised person on earth when you realize, "I am fulfilled. I am at peace. My cup runneth over, and I didn't even know this could be the life that is truly life!"

Refusing the allure of the shortcut is not easy. Initially, it takes much discipline to *think* our way through life, not to *feel* our way through. But the longer way around is where the riches of His life are to be discovered. The real desires of our heart are always worth the wait.

When you stand at the fork, facing the temptation to take the cultural shortcut instead of the longer path of patience and trust?

Will you resist your feelings and trust your Father, or will your feelings be your folly?

Hole 6

Desires of the Eyes or of the Heart?

"Delight yourself in the LORD and he will give you the desires of your heart."
Psalm 37:4

Satan's 3 D's: destroy… distract… and discourage. He will seek to distract us with an illusion and will then discourage us, regardless of whether we act on our lust or deny ourselves and go without. Lust takes us inevitably to, "I've got to have now!"

The path to peace is to scorn lusting and focus on God's promise: "Delight yourself in the LORD and he will give you the desires of your heart" (Psa. 37:4). Lust will never give you the desires of your heart, but your heavenly Father gladly will.

As a matter of fact, he will overwhelm you with the *true* desires of your heart if you allow him to. God's promise, which I have both observed and personally experienced, is that he can and will "do immeasurably more than all we ask or imagine" (Eph. 3:20).

I used to think this promise meant that if I was a good and sincere Christian, God would give me what I want. Now, I realize that I never knew what I truly wanted until I got out of the way and let him take charge of the desires of my heart.

When we take our focus off what we think we want—what we think will make us happy—and put it on the Lord, he will change our view of what we thought was so important. Those things will lose their allure and lose any hold it had on us. You'll be the most surprised person because you'll have the true desires of your heart, and you didn't even know that's what they were. You couldn't have imagined asking for what your Heavenly Father can deliver.

This is only when we refuse to indulge the illusions and see them for what they are: stupid, vaporous mirages.

While Satan wants to give us the C- life of distractions and discouragement, God is in the business of giving us the A+ "life that is truly life." He loves to fill us up. He thrives on it!

Hole 7

Narrowing Gates – Expanding Life

"Enter through the narrow gate. For wide is the gate and broad is the road
that leads to destruction, and many enter through it."
Matthew 7:13

Jesus cautions us to first find the narrow gate that leads to *Life* because he knows the current of this culture will sweep you right by it. After passing through that first, narrow gate to salvation, Jesus continues to invite you to look for even more gates as you progress in your spiritual journey.

These gates are the passageway deeper into the Kingdom. However, they get narrower the deeper we advance. You will have to drop the things in your life that won't fit through the narrowing gates and into the Kingdom. The incredibly wonderful surprise is that these narrowing gates lead to an ever-expanding life.

Narrower equals expansive? Yes!

Okay, let's get specific. If you want to keep advancing with Jesus towards the top, you will find it necessary to bump your trajectory from time to time because you will always plateau at some point. Let's say you're not sure you're really growing spiritually, or maybe you've just flattened out. You're frustrated (I hope) and want more. How can you get off this plateau and bump your spiritual trajectory upward?

You have two choices: new activities or a new surrender. Taking on a more intense Bible Study, digging into a challenging Christian book, attending an overnight conference, taking on any of the spiritual disciplines—such as scripture memorization, solitude and silence, extended prayer, or fasting—can help to bump your trajectory upward.

Surrender *always* brings us to a narrow gate, and the challenge is, "Are we willing to 'slim down' by letting go of... surrendering... whatever it is God has lain on our hearts?" It is always hard when we face a narrow gate and must surrender and shed to get through it.

What about you? Could you surrender a 'preciously guarded' area of your life? It may be a habit: not so bad, terrible, or even good. One friend realized it was golf. For another, it was girls' night out. For yet another, it was a grudge, a refusal to forgive. It may be a relationship. It may be your stinginess with money. Maybe it's a heart attitude of resentment, judgment, or superiority. Or... gossip. Oops.

Only you know what it is for you. However, you *do* know. It is blocking your advance. Whatever it is, when you hear the Holy Spirit's conviction that it needs to go, will you listen and respond? Will you face that narrow gate and surrender? Or will you hear the serpent's voice instead: "Did God really say that? Oh, come on, that wasn't God. No need to bother about it. You're just fine." But, you're not.

God loves you so much he doesn't want to leave you the way you are, even though he loves you perfectly either way. It is his perfect love that invites you to do deeper.

Hole 8

The Mind Melt

"For although they knew God, they neither glorified him as God nor gave thanks to him, but their thinking became futile and their foolish hearts were darkened. Although they claimed to be wise, they became fools."
Romans 1:21-22

We have all witnessed major league collapses by both men and women in the past few years. Mistakes made that are devastating. My guess is that not one of them decided one day to step out and screw up their lives. They drifted into it, whatever their particular life-altering, neon light mistake was.

And it started with a... non-decision. "This one time is no big deal."

Every affair starts with a moment when both parties know they are crossing an unhealthy line. Every embezzler starts with the promise, "Just this one time. I'll pay it back." Every alcoholic, drug addiction, porn addiction, or tax crime starts with a small step. Yet we don't pull back. And the downward spiral begins. Then one day it's, "How did this happen? What were they thinking?"

"Oh, that's not me. I'm not *that* bad." Maybe not. Maybe you've avoided the neon light collapse. But have you drifted into the C- life? Whether a front page meltdown or just a blasé spiritual fog, separation from God is not a matter of degree. He is either in you, or you are lost.

Our minds are sponges, absorbing what we see and hear. If we are sloppy with what we allow into our minds, we will suffer. Just as our bodies suffer with too much junk food, our minds are malnourished with the waste of this culture. How much time do you spend on email, surfing the internet, or watching TV? Maybe you're truly surfing and watching to enhance your mind, but more than likely, it's a mindless medley of mediocrity. We have two choices:

We can decide not to decide, and the mind will absorb both the vapor of this culture as well as its trash. For men, it starts with soft porn, a ridiculous oxymoron: Victoria's Secret, racy e-mail photos, or an internet site. For women, just take your pick from the myriad of magazines shouting out sure cures for your fashion, your weight, and your sex life.

Or, we can be prudent and purposeful about replenishing our minds with positive and spiritually uplifting thoughts and information. We can be prudent about repelling the trash with which we are constantly bombarded.

Ask yourself: "Will this enhance my mental and spiritual life, or will it inhibit it? Am I absorbing light or darkness? Three minutes, three days, or three weeks from now… will I be glad I have added this as a companion in my mind?

If you're not decisive about guarding your mind, the broad current of this mindless culture will wash you down river to either destruction or just the C- life. But if we are discerning and guard a narrow gate to our minds, we find the A+ "Life that is truly Life."

Hole 9

My Treasure Made Me Do It

"Above all else, guard your heart, for it is the wellspring of life."
Proverbs 4:23

What do Kobe Bryant, Michael Vick, Senator Larry Craig, Thomas Ravenel, the Enron executives, Jim and Tammy Faye Baker, Richard Nixon, and Bill Clinton (with Monica) have in common? With their *activities* being so widely varied, is it possible to find a common denominator? I think so.

Simply put, they were mastered by their treasures. Therefore, even though they may not have seen it that way at the time; they were in hot pursuit of their hearts' desires.

Now, can we find a common *treasure* in such a diversity of personalities? What kind of treasure could Kobe chasing the chambermaid, Michael chasing the dogs, Larry chasing men in the locker room, or Tommy chasing a cocaine high possibly have in common? Two mindsets:

First, "I deserve more."

Second, "This will make me happy because I have no real peace."

At some point, they had to ask themselves, "What was I thinking?" They were thinking one or both of the above.

What is your treasure? What *do* you treasure? Make no mistake about it. You will pursue your treasures. Jesus made it clear that our heart is where our treasures are because the heart is *the wellspring of life*.

What is the source for *your* heart? Are you in hot pursuit of the ultimate treasure: an ever-deepening relationship with Jesus? Or are you driven by treasures that master you… and deliver no peace?

Jesus promised, "Whoever believes in me, as the Scripture has said, streams of living water will flow from within him" (John 7:38). Are positive streams of living water flowing from within your heart out to those around you, or is your heart mastered by and *feeding on* the treasures of our culture?

Hole 10

Guard Rails

"Continue to work out your salvation with fear and trembling, for it is God who works in you to will and to act according to his good purpose."
Philippians 2:12

Perhaps you have a weakness, and you have repeatedly failed to conquer it. You've tried really hard with multiple attempts at rigid self-discipline. You've taped reminders and inspirational quotes on your mirror or in your car. You've even tried praying! But to no avail. You've made no progress.

It still has you... mastered.

We might be talking about a bad habit, physical or mental. Perhaps you smoke too much, drink too much, dip too much, or cuss, lie, cheat, gossip, condescend, judge, or lust... whew.

Like the Apostle Paul, you cry out, "I do not understand what I do. For what I want to do I do not do, but what I hate I do" (Rom. 7:15).

You need a guardrail. Because no matter how much you try to keep it between the lines, this issue, this weakness, has you mastered. It's causing you to behave like a drunken driver in your moment of weakness, and you keep ending up in a ditch.

I know a man who was fed up with his own aggressive driving and the resulting frustration with all the "idiot drivers" in his way. So he wrote a $100 check to a trusted friend and said, "You have my word, before God, the next time I drive that way you get the $100. And any time after that, I'll write you another check." He drives with much more peace now.

I know another man who sensed that he was drifting toward a pornography problem. He wrote a check to a trusted friend, and with a similar vow, he said, "You keep the $5,000 check if I ever do it again." Eight years later, he says he's never even been tempted. (He simply cannot *afford* to be.)

I know a woman who just couldn't quit smoking. She took a similar action.

Okay, I'm guessing about now you're either thinking, "Sam has slipped a mental disc," or, "But where is God in all this? Why aren't these people praying for the power of the Holy Spirit to deliver them?" They have. But they keep failing. Now, they are adhering to God's directive to do their part, as well as looking to him for strength.

The people described above are "working out their salvation" with protective and prohibitive guardrails. They are looking to God to work in them "to will and to act according to his good purpose." These men and women were tired of defeat, slavery to their weakness. They finally took definitive action to free themselves.

Guardrails are not my idea, and I'm not trying to be a restricting legalist about it. I'm following God's lead. Do you need a guardrail somewhere in your life? Yes, you do.

Hole 11

Guardrail Specifications

"A prudent man sees danger and takes refuge, but the simple keep going and suffer for it. In the paths of the wicked lie thorns and snares, but he who guards his soul stays far from them."
Proverbs 22:3

A friend of mine visited Niagara Falls and told me about a particular rock out-cropping that provided spectacular views of the falls. He said there was a guardrail erected about 15 feet back from the edge with a warning sign that says, "Beware! Thirty-eight people have fallen to their death."

Yet, every year, someone goes over the railing to… get closer to the edge. What is their thought process?

"It won't happen to me."

"I'm different and special."

"Just this one time."

"A little closer won't hurt anything."

We need to place guardrails in areas we know we are weak, or tempted, or have repeatedly failed before. And we do not place them right on the edge. No, we place them far enough back that even if we bump into them, the damage will not be catastrophic.

However, the specifications for a guardrail must include some degree of pain, or they will be meaningless. And they also must be solid, with detailed specs, and with no wiggle-room for rationalization.

I would guess that most dads aren't real big on their teenage daughters being in a house with a boy alone. We dads wouldn't say, "Now honey, you can be in the house, and you can go in his bedroom, just don't get in the bed." No, we would say, "I'm locking you in our house until you're 43!" (Just kidding… Slightly.)

A recently divorced man was telling me that he was seeing a woman, and he wanted to avoid the whole sex thing with her. I asked him what his guardrail was. He replied, "We are going no farther than a glass of wine on the sofa. No bedroom stuff at all." That's not a guardrail, that's an invitation.

We need guardrails primarily because in the moment, when we are struggling with whether or not to do it, say it, or yell it, our cost-benefit analysis is skewed. Looking back, we see clearly the long-term cost of such behavior is far greater than any short-term benefit. The problem is that in the moment, we are only thinking of the short-term benefit, with barely a nod to any cost at all.

I know a man who set up a "cuss" jar as a guardrail. A woman I know put a gossip jar in her kitchen: $10 goes in the jar each time, in front of her children. Another person promised to call her mother-in-law (oh my) each time she snaps at her husband or children. Another vowed no golf for a month if he is ever on his cellphone when his children get in the car.

Guardrails help keep us "walking in the light" to the A+ Life.

God will show you where. The specifications and installation are up to you.

Hole 12

High-Five or Utter Contempt?

*"For our struggle is not against flesh and blood, but against the rulers,
against the authorities, against the powers of this dark world and
against the spiritual forces of evil in the heavenly realms"*
Ephesians 6:12

Jesus saw God everywhere. His teachings only make sense in his context of a God-saturated world. Otherwise, they are far, far too lofty to attain.

King David saw God everywhere, too. He filtered everything coming his way through a lens of God everywhere and God already there. Except... when he didn't. Unlike Jesus, but like us, David could ease God out of the picture when his presence was inconvenient. Not when something or someone like Goliath was coming at him, but oh so quickly when something or someone like Bathsheba was.

The prophet Nathan sought to make David aware of the magnitude of his actions with a reminder that, from God's perspective, he didn't just behave poorly. No, from God's perspective, David despised him (2 Sam. 12:9).

We would say, "But no, Father, I wasn't despising *you* when I did that. I was just allowing myself a little indulgence. I meant nothing against you. Please don't take it personally." Apparently, he does.

When I *used* to sin, my main concern was not being caught and exposed. Nowadays, I don't really sin; like everyone else in this vapid culture, it's more like, "Mistakes were made." Nobody really sins. That's so Old Testament.

But if I am exposed, I'm first and foremost remorseful that I got caught. Then, I'm remorseful that I have to humble myself and grovel with an apology. But rarely do I think as David did, "I have sinned against the LORD" (Psa. 51:4).

But here's the thing: David didn't just forget about God's presence; he forgot about the presence of God's enemies as well. Nathan now ups the cosmic ante with a reminder to David that "you have made the enemies of the LORD show utter contempt" (2 Sam. 12:14). "The enemies of the LORD... show utter contempt? What? Who?"

I picture a stadium or arena of sorts. We are all "playing" out our lives in full view of God and Jesus, but also in full view of Satan and his cronies. God loves you; Satan hates God. To whom shall I give the victory?

God reminds us, "For our struggle is not against flesh and blood, but against the rulers, against the authorities, against the powers of this dark world and against the spiritual forces of evil in the heavenly realms" (Eph. 6:12).

It is? I thought it was just me doing my own thing, making "mistakes" but no big deal. Apparently, it is.

In this arena of life, will I give God and Jesus the high-five celebration, or will I "make the enemies of the LORD show utter contempt" for my Heavenly Father? To whom shall I give the high-five victory?

Hole 13

The Good Life

"Everything is permissible for me—but not everything is beneficial. Everything is permissible for me—but I will not be mastered by anything."
1 Corinthians 6:12

We enjoy obtaining and hoarding our treasures more than the treasure itself. I've found that, often, our treasures are our idea of what *The Good Life* is all about.

I'd like to ask you to stop for a moment and envision your image of *The Good Life*. We all have an image, a vision of what it would be like. Is yours colored by our culture or by Jesus' Way? Is it founded on what everybody else has and is doing, or can you see through the fog to what is the Truth?

I believe most of us have a skewed image of *The Good Life*. How could we not?

Where would we find the right examples to seek? TV? That vivaciously cute blond in the car commercials says, "You really can have it all at McKinney Dodge." Can I? Will she be there to help me find it all? My image of *The Good Life* is to have her as my wife. Oh, and she's to keep doing those commercials because part of my image is a wife that is an all-star, so my friends would envy me. We'd share a big, brick house near Crescent Avenue. Our three postcard kids would be great athletes, good in school, well-mannered, and popular in the right social circles—as would we, of course. Everyone—who counts—would think I'm a great guy: successful, smart, funny and yes, still cool.

Well, I used to think that way. I was *mastered* by it. It led me to pursue choices that I regret. Here's the catch about being mastered by skewed images of *The Good Life*:

First, we'll do what it takes to try to get it, often ignoring the consequences.

Second, if we don't get it, we'll feel like failures—or at a minimum, less *valuable*.

136

Jesus was big on *The Good Life*. He said He's come to give it to us. He called it the Abundant Life. Now, here's how I see the Abundant, Good Life: being able to say, "No thanks, I'm full," when faced with a temptation, whether it be outright evil or just a "C-."

You see, I really want God's will for my life, instead of just being willing to accept it with gritted teeth. I don't want to control the outcome or manipulate things because I'd really rather Him control it.

And I now have: freedom from the tyranny of what others think, and the freedom to live God's way. And that's *The Good Life!*

Hole 14

Master Money

"Watch out! Be on your guard against all kinds of greed..."
Luke 12:15

We put guardrails up in the areas of our lives where we know we have a weakness. We put guardrails up to protect us from being mastered by anything: bad habits, bad heart attitudes, or whatever else might have a mastery over you. Jesus seemed to think we need a major guardrail against money being our Master.

Are you greedy? I am. Or maybe I'd like to say I used to be. I'm sure that's more accurate. The love of money is such a devious fiend. It always has the potential to regain control and enslave me again.

God warns us about the trap of money well over two thousand times throughout the Scriptures, more than mentions of heaven or hell. Did you ever stop to think, why? Does God want your money? Does God need your money?

Or, does God know you will end up worshiping something, and if it isn't Him, money will be at the top of the list. The path to the A+ Life is to have Jesus as your Lord and Master, seeking him first, and kicking money to the back of the line.

The only guardrail solution I have found to be sure money does not have any kind of mastery over me is to give it away, generously. If you have another plan, please share it with me. Don't get me wrong. I won't stop giving money away because it's too much fun, and it is way too satisfying and rewarding.

But if you have another plan, I'd be interested. And, I would be... skeptical. Because no one thinks they are greedy, and most *think* they are generous.

Jesus said, "The eye is the lamp of the body. If your eyes are good (meaning, "generous without reserve"), your whole body will be full of light. But if your eyes are bad (meaning, "double, duplicitous"), your whole body will be full of darkness" (Matt. 6:22-23).

Here's what this looks like. A friend sends out a request to two friends, asking for financial assistance to help a young man get a leg up in life. The rich man, the one with "double, duplicitous" eyes, will likely respond, "What, are we supposed to save the world? How do I know this is legit? What if this young man is just a loafer? Why should I give my hard-earned money?"

Can't you just see his squinty eyes? Suspicious… duplicitous… enslaved.

But the one with "generous without reserve" eyes responds, "Yes! What a wonderful opportunity to personally invest in a young man's life!"

The difference is startling and scary. Full of light. Full of dark suspicion.

There is a freedom that comes from generosity. Financial freedom. Freedom from slavery. A joyous, enriching, yes even fun way to live!

How can I be sure that I'm not mastered by money? I'm going to setup a guardrail against greed by giving away generously. And you?

Hole 15

Tempted!—The Hot Cookie

"When the woman saw that the fruit of the tree was good for food and pleasing to the eye, and also desirable for gaining wisdom, she took some and ate it. Then the eyes of both of them were opened, and they realized they were naked"
Genesis 3:6-7

My friends have been having trouble with their one-year-old son, Will. It seems he's been causing all kinds of trouble for them: talking back, disrupting the peace of the house, and even blatantly disobeying them. Last week, while trying to get a piping hot cookie out of the hot oven, he knocked over a family heirloom, shattering it to pieces and burning his hand in the process. His parents asked if I would sit down with Will for a counseling session. We agreed, and we met the next day.

"Okay, Sam, let's just set the record straight," Will stated before I had a chance to engage him. "I don't want to be here. I didn't really do anything that bad. My parents just don't understand me, and they sure don't know what it's like to be a one-year-old in today's world. Back in their day, it was easy to go along with all the rules. But things are different now, and I have to take care of #1, first."

He popped his pacifier into his mouth and glared at me defiantly.

Hoping to defuse his hostility, I said, "Well, why don't you tell me what happened. Start with their rules. Did your parents tell you not to eat any of the cookies in the oven? Did they warn you that the oven was hot and you would get burned?"

"Yeah, but you see, I knew they were just throwing out an arbitrary rule, just to keep me in-line. They do it all the time. All these rules and for no apparent reason. Always lurking around to scold me if I break one of them. They may say they love me, but they sure must enjoy controlling me and denying me anything that's really fun. I don't call that love. It's my life, and I know what's best for me."

"But, you got burned. I know that had to hurt," I said trying to reason with him. "And the vase is now shattered. It can never be put back to the way it was before. Couldn't you see the hurt in your mother's eyes?"

"I wanted that cookie," he continued. "I needed that cookie to be happy." His face slowly started dropping as his gaze shifted to the floor. Then, defiantly, he said, "I *deserved* that cookie. So, I took it!" With that, he pulled his shirt up over his face and started crying.

I could see he felt shame for his actions. Now, he knew—for the first time—the difference between good and evil. He was exposed and hiding behind his self-assurance.

"Was the cookie really worth it after all, Will? Are you glad you trusted yourself and got your way instead of trusting your parents and their desire to protect you? Are you still so sure they don't love you perfectly?"

Does this scenario sound familiar in your life? Don't we often act like Will?

Hole 16

Esau

"What good will it be for a man if he gains the whole world, yet forfeits his soul?
Or what can a man give in exchange for his soul?"
Matthew 16:26

E sau got tricked, twice, by his younger twin, Jacob. In the South, we would start any conversation about Esau with, "You know Esau, bless his heart..." Southern Christians have discovered that we can freely gossip about anyone, as long as we start with, "Bless their heart..."

Okay, so Esau does deserve a bad rap, at the beginning. But what you may not know is he turns out to be one of the huge heroes of the Old Testament. In sports jargon, "He's the best player you've never heard of." His story can serve us well as to what not to do, as well as what to do, how to live one's life after being knocked backwards.

Young Esau comes in from hunting, and he's hungry... famished! The aroma from Jacob's stew overwhelms him, and he begs for a bowl. That wily rabbit Jacob, sensing his advantage, agrees, but only if Esau swaps his birthright for the stew. Esau cries out, "I am about to die. What good is the birthright to me?" (Gen. 25:32)

Stop the presses. Did you hear what was actually going on in Esau's mind? "If I don't get this, I cannot be happy?" Have you ever said the same thing? Sure you have... just in different words, couched in some logical, adult-sounding rationalization. How many times have we thought to ourselves, "I *have* to have this... it must turn out this way... I must control this... I cannot live without this?" Underlying all of this is the idea that "only with *this* can I be happy."

And so, like Esau, you bargained away your birthright: your self-respect, your word, your kindness, your virginity, your physical or emotional health. You took a shortcut. You fudged. You "white-lied." You got involved in and stayed in a negative relationship. You starting cheating on your taxes, your business, your spouse, or your God... all because you thought you would die if you didn't get what you had to have to be happy.

No, you wouldn't have died without it. But sadly, your soul died a little with it.

Hole 17

The Tyranny of Busyness

"Come to me, all you who are weary and burdened, and I will give you rest."
Matthew 11:28-29

Imagine, if you will, another weekly strategy session between Satan and his demons as they plot to destroy our lives. Satan sighs, stands up, and looks around the table at each demon. He says, "Listen, you're getting carried away with these grand schemes. I know the neon light sins like drug addiction and pornography are fun, and they make such a mess of the humans' lives, but they only work on certain people. I want you to remember what our goal: to hurt God. Period."

He pauses for effect. "Whatever schemes we pursue, the end goal is always to get back at God. What better way to hurt him than to hurt his precious children? Attacking and embarrassing them is fun, so when you can incite them into big flame-out sins, have at it. But, they often bounce back from those types of failures. Often, their family and friends circle around to help, and the whole thing goes to naught because when it's over, God has once again trumped us and worked good out of a bad situation."

"No, we must stick to our first and primary strategy, our bread and butter: busyness. Busyness has proven to be consistently effective. The humans admire busyness, they feel good being busy, and they look important being busy," Satan says, shaking his head.

"I know!" exclaims one of the older demons. "Over the years, I've learned that if I can just keep mine busy, I keep them distracted, and my job is easy after that. Think about it, I've got them missing God altogether, or they're missing that so-called A+ 'Life that is truly life' God is always promising them, and they don't even have a clue."

At this point, one of the younger demons coughs and says meekly, "I have a confession to make, and I know I'm going to get in a lot of trouble for this. But, my guy joined a church. I've failed and feel like such an imbecile."

Almost in unison the older demons said, "Are you kidding? Church might be the safest place to have him. Just get him busy at church, and keep him distracted with all there is to do with the committees and the projects. Remind him how important this all makes him feel. You'll have nothing to worry about after that."

"Yes," Satan exclaims as he slams his fist down on the table, "You older guys are doing great. Keep it up. We even have them measuring their self-worth by how busy they are. Can you believe how stupid they must be? So, learn this, above all else. And never forget our motto: 'If you can't make 'em bad, make 'em busy!'"

Remember that your best defense against this scheme is to come to Jesus. He will give you rest.

Hole 18

Sin & Other Fun Things

"Whatever you do, do it for the glory of God. Do not cause anyone to stumble..."
1 Corinthians 10:31-32

Are all sins equal? Yes and no. Can something be a sin for me and not for you? Yes. Can something be a sin for me today and not a sin at a later date, all else being equal? Yes. Can refusing to do something be a sin? Yes. Am I right if I have done nothing wrong? Maybe, but maybe not.

I'm not looking to brow-beat you today about your sins; I'll let Jesus do that. However, I'd like for you to think about the literal meaning of the word, *sin*: "To miss the mark." Then, think about how this applies to Jesus' desire for us to have and to live the A+ "Life that is truly life."

God is all about protecting, not prohibiting. Please don't miss that. He's about freedom, not restriction. God gives us a remarkable perspective on this, which goes far beyond the elementary question of, "Is this a sin?" We should be asking ourselves the following three questions:

First, will this gain mastery over me? Paul writes, "Everything is permissible for me... but not everything is beneficial. Everything is permissible for me... but I will not be mastered by anything" (1 Cor. 6:12).

Second, could this have a negative impact on someone around me? Paul explains, "Be careful, however, that the exercise of your freedom does not become a stumbling block to the weak" (1 Cor. 8:9).

Third, will this make a positive impact on someone else's life? "Everything is permissible... but not everything is beneficial. Everything is permissible...but not everything is constructive. Nobody should seek his own good, but the good of others." (1 Cor. 10:23-24)

As a grown-up, I might say, "Staying up late and watching a lot of TV are not sins. Smoking is not a sin. Getting *tipsy* just once a week is not a sin. Hunting on my weekends is not a sin. Girls night out is not a sin. Playing golf when I could be with my family is not a sin. Working all the time is not a sin."

To all this God might say, "Maybe, maybe not. But, is it beneficial? Does it have a hold on you? Might it be a stumbling block for anyone else—maybe even your own family?" These are the A+ Life questions.

If we have to ask if something is a sin for us, it probably is. It's time we got out of the schoolyard sandbox of, "Is it wrong? Will God get mad at me?" We need to move to a higher place of walking in the Light.

"Is this walking in the Light?" That's a far richer perspective when faced with the choice to be kind or to be right... when faced with *reacting* in fear and emotion or responding in faith and trust... when rationalizing, "It's not personal, it's business"... or when my choices revolve around me-first, others after that.

Make your decisions on the basis of, "Is this walking in the Light?"

About the Author

Sam Hunter is the host of South Carolina's Christian radio talk show, *721 Live*, which helps people to apply the Bible to their everyday lives. He has produced two DVD curriculum series: *Contentment: The Path to Peace* and *Fear: Do you React in Fear or Respond in Faith?*

After operating his own real estate and construction company for twenty years, Sam founded *721 Ministries*, which provides Christian coaching and teaching for hundreds of businessmen each week.

In addition to speaking to men's groups weekly, Sam is frequently invited to speak to mixed and couples groups at various churches and retreats. He also speaks to Fellowship of Christian Athletes (FCA) groups at high schools and colleges.

Sam was educated and trained as a structural design engineer at Georgia Tech and Clemson University.

He now resides in Greenville, SC.